Contents

Cover photo: *The Supper at Emmaus,* by Diego Velázquez. The Metropolitan Museum of Art.

Introduction

I spent considerable time at the hospital with my mother during the last days of her life. One afternoon as I walked into her room, she held up her hand. A small clip was attached to her index finger and connected to a machine that measured the oxygen level in her blood. She was convinced its purpose was to send her a signal. "A special baby is to be born. As soon as that happens, this clip will let me know it's time for me to die," she said.

I could not convince her otherwise. Who was I to argue? She needed a sign of hope before she could let go. Interestingly, when we called people to tell them of her passing, one family whom she dearly loved informed us of the birth of a beautiful granddaughter that very evening. Perhaps my mother sensed a truth more profound than any medical instrument could measure.

Mother wanted to experience God's "Yes!" in this world before she was ready to embrace the next life. Her experience was really quite scriptural. The psalmist wrote, "I believe that I shall see the goodness of the LORD in the land of the living" (Psalm 27:13). Genesis 1 tells of God's great affirmation, the act of creation in which "Yes!" came forth repeatedly from God's mouth. The last word in the Bible (Revelation 22:21) is "Amen," which can be loosely translated, "O, Yes!"

What marvelous stories there are between "In the beginning when God..." and that final "Amen" to John's amazing vision. Included in the biblical record are tales of sins too numerous to count, of astounding failures, of frequent wars, of violence, even of betrayal. Yet the overarching word is one of promise. God's love is with us from start to finish. God's grace is lavished upon us. We are a people of hope with tidings of hope to tell.

Let us approach these Lent/Easter lectionary texts with hopefulness and eager expectation. Though God has sent forth a resounding "Yes!" to a new millennium, we might be tempted to retreat to the comfort of things familiar. Like those Hebrew people and their forty years of wandering, we might likely wish sometimes to return to our old ways. We might muse, "O, I've studied these same texts before. They come around every three years, don't they? And I seem to remember listening to sermons based on them from several different preachers." Trusting rather in the Spirit's fresh inspiration, we can say to these passages, "Welcome, old friends! It's good to see you again. What new insights, what surprising blessings do you hold for me?"

God's "Yes!" is forever creative, full of unbounded growth potential, and overflowing with tidings of hope.

A Holy Bath and a Moist Faith

Scriptures for Lent:
The First Sunday
Genesis 9:8-17
1 Peter 3:18-22
Mark 1:9-15

The area of the western United States I live in is nearly desert. The hills are dotted with sagebrush and dry grasses. Jackrabbits and rattlesnakes abound. By late summer, everything is a shade of brown, right down to the edges of streams and rivers that meander by. Even weeds struggle for survival, and thick layers of dust blanket the entire landscape. Where irrigation is possible and water touches the soil, however, the change is dramatic. Fields are carpeted in lush green; fruit trees produce abundant yields; golf courses and recreational sites offer oases in the dryness and heat.

Water is God's gift to the parched earth and to the thirsty soul. The waters of baptism are to humanity what soaking rains are to the earth: refreshing, renewing, life-giving. The lectionary passages for this Sunday in Lent focus on the beauty and power of water.

Genesis recounts the story of the great flood and of how Noah, his family, and all living creatures were saved from the water by the water. God took the initiative and covenanted with creation to never again destroy by flood the life that teems upon this planet. God sealed the promise with a rainbow, a visible reminder both to God and humanity. Peter offers a reprise of water's power to bring about salvation in the time of Noah, then applies it to the cleansing, sacramental qualities of baptism in Jesus Christ. The Gospel lection continues this theme with Jesus' baptism, his testing in the wilderness, and his proclamation of the coming of God's Realm. The old covenant God made with Noah finds its completion in the new covenant inaugurated by God's own Son.

The New Testament passages contain a rich understanding of Christian baptism. They provide us with an opportunity to immerse ourselves in the mystery and profound power of the sacrament. They remind us that baptism is much more than a minor ordinance or a brief digression from our usual patterns of corporate worship. Baptism is God-ordained, spiritually potent, and life changing.

One Sunday morning I was baptizing a two-year-old and his mother. The child was worried about what I was going to do with that water. So before sprinkling him, I let him briefly play with it. He then willingly received his baptism. Next his mother knelt beside the font. Before I could put my hand into the bowl, the child leaned from his father's arms; dipped his small hand into the water; and very gently, sweetly, baptized the top of his mother's head. Joy and happy laughter filled the sanctuary. My own triune application of water seemed almost redundant. Truly her baptism was of love and the Spirit. So also may our journey of faith be throughout this season of Lent.

SEALED WITH A RAINBOW
Genesis 9:8-17

When floods occur anywhere on this earth, I watch the news reports with fascination and great compassion. I can only imagine what the feelings must be for those who have lost their homes and cherished possessions. There must be a sense of hopelessness as the victims of nature's destruction contemplate the overwhelming process of rebuilding. Our human efforts seem puny in the face of such irresistible forces. Even a minor inconvenience, like a clogged sewer drain causing a backup into the basement, can be quite unsettling. For a while, all the usual patterns and comforts are gone. We seem to expend the vast majority of our energy and resources simply trying to cope with the crisis.

It must have been much the same for Noah and his family. After nearly eleven months on board a crowded, smelly, and most likely leaky boat, the waters finally receded. They threw open the doors of the ark and stood once more on dry ground. But what a mess must have greeted them! Mud would have been caked on everything. They no doubt faced the cleaning of massive debris piles and doing battle with hordes of insects. After the daunting task of building the ark and enduring those noisy, sleepless nights upon the flood waters, came the challenge of putting the pieces back together again.

God, who is full of kindness and mercy, took pity on Noah and made a promise: "I establish my covenant with you, that never again shall all flesh be cut off by the waters of a flood, and never again shall there be a flood to destroy the earth" (Genesis 9:11). God provided Noah and his kin with the necessary will and energy to proceed with the hard work that lay ahead. This divine covenant was all-inclusive. It extended to every living creature as well as to all future generations. There was no exclusionary language; no fine print. God entered into this commitment freely. The initiative for such a covenantal relationship rested solely with God.

Whenever thick clouds covered the earth again, Noah and his descendents quite likely would have glanced anxiously overhead. Could this be the beginning of another downpour, was another flood soon to follow? But God added a special touch, a gift of reassurance: "I have set my bow in the clouds, and it shall be a sign of the covenant between me and the earth" (verse 13). The primary purpose of the rainbow was to remind God of this binding and everlasting covenant. A secondary, yet significant reason for the rainbow was to bring a sense of security and peace to human life. From that time forth the bow was to serve as a visible, glorious reminder of God's patient love and unwavering devotion to the whole of creation.

The scientific explanation of a rainbow hardly does it justice. It is described as a natural optical phenomenon produced by dispersion, reflection, and refraction of the sun's rays, requiring an enormous number of water droplets at any given moment in the atmosphere. While that may be an accurate physical description, it cannot begin to account for a rainbow's surpassing beauty. We humans are unable to appreciate its full radiance because of our limited vision. Neither can we fathom the complete range and extent of God's grace. Yet whatever small portion of divine love we do experience within our hearts and minds is sufficient to sustain our commitment, loyalty, and thanksgiving to our Creator.

This is the same God who brings forth blossoms and butterflies, sunsets and waterfalls, roses and moonlight. God's love is expressed in commandments, promises, prophets, poetry, and songs and with marvelous splashes of color arching the sky. God, of course, does not forget this intimate relationship with humanity between rainbows. God is not just the God of rains and floods, of trouble and crisis. God is revealed in sunlight and in beautiful days. God is our constant companion, our strength for every step of life's journey.

Noah's close connection to God enabled him to live out his many years with courage and hope. There were more tough times ahead. Nevertheless, Noah's offspring became the basis for the nations that spread abroad throughout the earth. What a blessed combination is a faithful person and a patient, loving God!

What are the foundational promises of God on which your life is based?

In moments of trouble and crisis, how has God offered you hope?

Have you been blessed with any special, visible signs of God's loving, reassuring presence?

After the floods have receded, after the trials and griefs are past, messes are usually left behind to clean. What practical and spiritual resources, both personal and within the faith community, can help in this essential process of rebuilding?

SOAKING IN THE WATER, BASKING IN THE SON LIGHT
1 Peter 3:18-22

In his wonderfully poetic New Testament translation in contemporary English, *The Message*, Eugene H. Peterson provides a refreshing and insightful glimpse into our Epistle lesson. We recall how Noah endured the ridicule of neighbors in addition to the demanding and exacting work of building the ark. Reminding us that God waited patiently while Noah and his crew constructed the equivalent of an ocean-going cargo vessel, Peter points out that only a few, eight humans to be exact, were saved. They were, says our text, "...saved FROM the water BY the water. The waters of baptism do that for you, not by washing away dirt from your skin but by presenting you through Jesus' resurrection before God with a clear conscience. Jesus has the last word on everything and everyone, from angels to armies. He's standing right alongside God, and what he says goes."[1]

This passage in First Peter offers us opportunities to rethink our attitudes about the Lenten season. The common, prevailing view of Lent is as a time of intense personal discipline and serious repentance. It has not always been so. In the early church, the forty days of Lent were used as preparation for new converts to receive Holy Baptism. While not neglecting the penitential aspects of the season, we should also emphasize other important Lenten themes such as conversion, baptism, and new life in Christ.

Daniel T. Benedict, Jr., in his book *Come to the Waters*, calls us to celebrate the beginnings of faith during Lent and in particular on this first Sunday. "During these Sundays," he writes, "Jesus is no slumping cross bearer. He is the one about whom every hearer must make a fresh assessment and response. This is not a season to focus on ourselves and our efforts; it is a season of journey in the company of One who is a mystery and a sign of God for us. Trust the gospel and the work of the Holy Spirit to work conversion in the people."[2] If you listen carefully, you may just hear Peter say a rousing "Amen!" to these thought-provoking words. There is a sense of urgency about shaping and sharing a new paradigm, not only for Lent and the baptismal rite, but for the nature of the church as well. By reading between the lines, you can feel that same urgency in Peter's words. A world-changing event, the death and resurrection of Jesus had occurred some years earlier. It was now time for people to respond with faith, to be converted, to be baptized, and to accept the complete authority of Christ.

Some of the same compelling reasons for immediate action as those of the first century are applicable to our day. Like Peter and his contemporaries, we cannot presume that everyone is acquainted with Jesus Christ, even in superficial or casual ways. Benedict addresses this critical issue: "Congregations can no longer assume that the culture has engaged people in any significant contact with Christian tradition. More and more persons are starting from ground zero as they search for the meaning, love, and belonging that prompts them to start out on a journey of seeking God and conversion. They come to churches with little, if any, previous experience with a Christian group or tradition."[3]

Becoming familiar with texts such as 1 Peter 3 is a helpful and solid place to begin. Verses 18 and 19, for example, give us the foundation for such urgency. Christ endured suffering "in order to bring you to God. He was put to death in the flesh, but made alive in the spirit." Can we not agree that people in today's world have a desperate need to know and trust God, to be made alive in the spirit?

Our response to God's grace is to accept it joyfully through baptism, to obey God's moral laws, and to recognize Christ's authority

in our lives. These imply the necessity of belonging to a community of believers. The Christian faith is not designed for isolated individuals. The Lone Ranger made good copy as a rugged individual in the Old West. Unfortunately, it seems many of his descendants are still found in our churches today. God designed the Christian faith to be a corporate venture. Each of us is given strength, wisdom, and spiritual gifts. Yet we all stand in need of the church's support, correction, encouragement, and inspiration. We belong together. This is especially true for our understanding of baptism. The sacrament is often little more than a social event, a reason to dress up and have a party, or the desire to ensure its future listing in our obituary. We need to recover its central and sacramental place in the life of every vital congregation.

The resource *Come to the Waters* offers helpful, practical advice on how to balance individual spiritual needs during Lent and Easter with the activities of the whole body of Christ. The schedule of church life ought to be focused on the mystery of Christ's sacrifice. "Busyness should be set aside...." We should rather, "Focus on the means of grace; on praise; on the mystery of participation in Christ's death and resurrection in the sacraments; and in ministry to the poor, the suffering, and oppressed."[4] Moments of silence and quiet meditation are suggested as ways to allow the living Lord to deepen our faith. God, who waited patiently in the days of Noah, may well be waiting for us to become more receptive to the Holy Spirit's leading, to be willing to adopt new forms of worship, and to take baptism seriously. In short, God waits for us to accept that "Jesus has the last word on everything and everyone . . . and what he says goes."[5]

How does the fact that fewer people know the basics of the Christian faith impact your witnessing?

What personal indications do you have that there is a sense of urgency in sharing the good news of Jesus Christ?

In what specific ways can you help your congregation recover their role and responsibility for the sacrament of baptism?

Do you agree that we stand now at the brink of a great spiritual revival? Why or why not?

THE ENERGY AND EXCITEMENT OF NEW BEGINNINGS
Mark 1:9-15

Several parallels between the season of Lent and the experience of moving to a new home or area of the country may be found. Both require extensive planning and preparations, including getting rid of worn-out and no longer needed possessions. In the case of moving, we hold a yard sale and make numerous trips to the dump. In Lent we are asked to examine our inner life and to let go of outgrown and narrow theological views, to dump unloving attitudes and outmoded religious practices.

Moving to a new residence or through the weeks of Lent are both demanding ventures requiring a great deal of work and considerable amounts of anxiety. In both, change is the order of the day. The apostle Paul, who himself was almost constantly on the move, understood the feeling. He expressed the spiritual dimension of what happens in conversion when he wrote, "So if anyone is in Christ, there is a new creation: everything old has passed away; see, everything has become new!" (2 Corinthians 5:17). Changing apartments or houses may in fact be far easier than rapid growth in Christian faith. When undertaken with intentionality and seriousness, it poses a major challenge.

Why, though, should it be any different for us than it was for Jesus? Though he may have sensed that one day this moment would come, his actual leave-taking must have seemed rather sudden and abrupt. Daily contact with his mother and his Nazarene friends would quickly be replaced by fellowship with the disciples. The labor of crafting furniture and utensils by the art of carpentry would soon give way to shaping the hearts and souls of people. The comforts of home were to be left behind for a wandering existence with few creature comforts.

In order to prepare for this radical transition, Jesus first received baptism before being tested in the wilderness. Mark's Gospel vividly describes these scenes. Apparently an intense person, the Gospel writer says exactly what he means and little else, using only seven verses. Mark's language, perhaps like his personality, is filled with action. These few lines are packed with verbs. We get the distinct feeling that things are happening fast, that this is a decisive moment in history, and that we would do well to pay attention. It is sort of like driving through a small town where, if you go too fast or blink, you may miss it all.

As you read this passage in Mark, pause briefly after each of the three themes or paragraphs. Pretend there are rests in the text as in a musical score. Breathe deeply and meditate on what Jesus' baptism, temptation experience, and announcement of the Kingdom's arrival may have meant for him. This relatively short Gospel lesson packs an amazing amount of activity and history into a few verses. Give each event the attention it rightly deserves.

Jesus first presents himself to his cousin John at the River Jordan. Thoughtful Christians through the centuries have wondered why Jesus did so. John's baptism emphasized repentance, yet we believe Jesus was without sin (2 Corinthians 5:21). Perhaps its purpose was not for inner cleansing and forgiveness but for Jesus to feel connected to the Hebrew people, to identify with the holy nation to whom he was to minister. He may also have been preparing himself for his solitary temptation by establishing solidarity with other seekers of God's will, bonding with those in the land who were spiritually awake, who expected the Messiah's imminent arrival.

Whatever his motivations, Jesus' baptism was a watershed event. This decisive event set the direction for the rest of his life. In addition, Jesus' baptism confirmed for him his identity as God's Son. He received, if you will, parental approval. "And a voice came from heaven, 'You are my Son, the Beloved; with you I am well pleased' " (Mark 1:11). Jesus was thus emotionally and spiritually equipped for the testing that followed immediately. Like Noah and the rainbow, God's blessing included a visible symbol, a descending dove to represent peace and faithfulness.

As with our Savior, baptism is intended to be for us a power-packed, radical experience. Robin Maas, in *Living Hope: Baptism and the Cost of Christan Witness*, writes, "This holy bath changes us forever. It changes our name, our allegiance, and our destiny. It does indeed 'set us apart,' and from that moment on we are headed elsewhere."[6] From the moment of our baptism, our values are based on loving obedience to God and on loving service for our neighbors. Following that "holy bath," our hope for the future rises out of our hope in Christ, from trusting that God's grace will find a way.

Dan Benedict shares this bit of wisdom: "The flow of grace moves like a river. Grace respects the channel as long as the channel does not restrict the movement of grace. If there is resistance, grace will cut a new channel. In this sense, the grace of God will always be subversive of our blindness and our narrow agendas. Jesus Christ, flowing in attentiveness to all persons, cuts through the bureaucratic mazes that oppose his sovereign freedom. The straight path to love's ocean will finally win."[7]

Jesus was moistened by the waters of the Jordan, then thrust by the Spirit into the parched desert. Mark does not list any of the specifics of this forty-day ordeal. Rather, he tells us that Jesus had the companionship of wild beasts and that angels ministered to him. We too have times of testing, times when we live in arid, parched surroundings. Believing in Jesus Christ and/or having been baptized does not exempt us from such trials. Like Jesus, however, we are offered abundant spiritual resources, not only to endure the struggles but, in fact, to grow in faith. God is present in the refreshing waters of the river; in the peace and quiet of those high mountaintops; and in all those places in between, those uncharted, confusing, difficult areas of wilderness. We may be tested, but we never have to go through it alone. God is with us.

The deepest, most profound basis of our hope then lies in the astounding proclamation of Jesus that followed his temptation: "The time is fulfilled, and the kingdom of God has come near; repent, and believe in the good news" (Mark 1:15). This is not wishful thinking, some clever brand of escapist theology. Our hope has a solid foundation: nothing less than the eternal, unshakable realm of God. Eugene Peterson's translation of this verse is quite startling: "Time's up! God's kingdom is here. Change your life and believe the Message."[8]

God employs wonderfully kind and wise ways in nurturing us imperfect creatures. For instance, in life's every ending we experience God's new beginning. Each dawn is proof of that; so is the beauty of spring, the healing that follows grief, and resurrection after crucifixion. Here in Mark 1, the old covenant is about to yield to a new one. God is ready to give birth to a new order. There will be struggle and pain. The old system is not about to release its grip gracefully. The process of change will require God's patience and forgiveness in far greater measure than in the time of Noah. Ah, but the blessings, the joys, and the treasure of hope in our hearts will be beyond all human reckoning.

Though it might require thousands upon thousands of human years to reach its final culmination, the energy inherent in this kingdom of God movement will propel us forward. Indeed, it almost seems as though something or Someone is stirring up this power again. Could we be about to see what Jesus saw on his baptismal day, the very heavens torn apart and the Spirit descending? Let us hope and pray that for our hurting world it will happen soon.

Do you think, given the present state of world affairs, that hopefulness for the future is nothing more than wishful thinking? Or is it possible that hope might be based on solid and abiding spiritual principles?

When have you observed signs that the Spirit is again stirring in the church?

Do you, or do you not, feel a renewing of spiritual energy in your life and in the Christian community? Why?

Do you concur with Dan Bene-dict's comment that grace moves like a river and that "the straight path to love's ocean will finally win"?

The early church expected that God's Realm would come in completeness at any moment. It obviously did not. Do you have any idea why it has been delayed?

If you could set the timetable for the coming of the Kingdom, when would it occur?

---

[1]From *The Message*, by Eugene H. Peterson (NavPress, 1993); pages 491-92.

[2]From *Come to the Waters*, by Daniel T. Benedict, Jr. (Discipleship Resources, 1996); page 92.

[3]From *Come to the Waters*; page 16.

[4]From *Come to the Waters*; page 81.

[5]From *The Message*; page 492.

[6]From *Living Hope: Baptism and the Cost of Christian Witness*, by Robin Maas (Discipleship Resources, 1999); page 43.

[7]From *Come to the Waters*; page 51.

[8]From *The Message*; page 75.

Life's Unclenched Moments

In a delightfully refreshing book of poetic prayers, Ted Loder offers a petition to God entitled "Guide Me Into an Unclenched Moment."[1]

Gentle me,
Holy One,
into an unclenched moment.
    a deep breath,
    a letting go
        of heavy expectancies,
            of shriveling anxieties,
            of dead certainties,
    that, softened by the silence,
        surrounded by the light,
            and open to the mystery,
    I may be found by wholeness,
        upheld by the unfathomable,
        entranced by the simple,
            and filled with the joy
            that is you.

Many people in these stressful times live their lives from a clenched position. They are anxious, worried, usually expecting the worst. It is not the posture God wants for us. We are called to open our hearts, minds, and hands to God and to one another; to breathe deeply; to let go of self-centeredness; and to embrace God's gift of love. In their unique ways, each of this Sunday's Scripture lessons reminds us to be receptive, optimistic, and hopeful people.

Abram and Sarai (Genesis 17) expressed trust in God and graciously received new names from God. They believed the promise of the birth of a son and accepted the tremendous responsibilities that would surely follow. After their initial shock, they opened themselves to a future that would radically change their lives.

The apostle Paul reminded the Christian community in Rome that the promises made to Abraham and Sarah depended on faith, not on the law. Filled with hope, these two believed the promise of God and did not waver from it. They embraced God's plan and moved toward it with boldness and courage. Paul strongly stated that authentic life for those under the New Covenant comes by accepting through faith the saving, justifying love of Jesus Christ.

Our hope in Christ is genuine, Mark explains in an important narrative found in Chapter 8. A discourse between Jesus and Peter calls us to put first things first and includes the oft-quoted phrase, "Get thee behind me, Satan" (8:33, KJV). The realm of God requires our ultimate allegiance. Like our Lord, we are expected to give ourselves to others freely and without reservation, including the willingness to suffer for love's sake. Paradoxically, we discover our truest nature when we cease squeezing our hands around small, petty desires and learn to relax our grip, letting go and losing ourselves in God's great purposes.

The world tells us to be selfish, anxious, and defensive. According to popular wisdom, it is the only way to survive in such complicated and competitive times. But this Sunday, our three lectionary passages suggest otherwise. By having faith in God, by trusting in God's promises, and by following Jesus' example of sacrificial love, we find life's fullness and joy. We must unclench our human lives in order to gain the inner peace and eternal security we so earnestly desire.

NEW TIMES, NEW NAMES, NEW LIFE
Genesis 17:1-7, 15-16

I was thirty-four when our last child was born, and I felt as though I was getting a bit too old for diapers, late night feedings, and pacing the floor while holding a baby with colic. I vividly remember both how exciting and how tiring the experience was. What thoughts and feelings must Abram and Sarai have had when God said (loosely paraphrased), "O, by the way, don't call your wife Sarai any longer. She needs a new name to match yours. Sarah has a gentle and maternal sound to it, don't you think? After all, the two of you are going to have a son. I'm going to bless her and through the centuries make her offspring into a great nation with great leaders." Abraham and Sarah were one hundred and ninety years old respectively.

Talk about a drastic change of lifestyle! Recent studies indicate that the birth of a child, even during normal childbearing years, produces a major crisis. It may be a happy event, but a child is quite demanding. In fact, the birth of a child, along with the death of a spouse, getting married, and being fired from one's job, falls in the top dozen reasons for personal crises. Other than falling on his face and laughing (Genesis 17:17), Abraham handled it well. Apparently, so did Sarah, although her laughter (18:9-15) may have bordered on the hysterical.

When God appeared to Abram, the first item of business was to enter into a covenantal relationship (17:2). Everything that was to follow depended upon this faithful bond. On God's side of the agreement were a pledge of fruitfulness to Abraham and Sarah (17:6); a promise of everlasting continuity and stability (17:7); and a gift of land, Canaan, as a perpetual holding for them and their descendants (17:8). Note how the voice of God dominates this entire text. Abraham showed great respect and proved to be a good listener, while God did all the talking. The initiative for this divine-human covenant rests solely with God.

Our lectionary passage does not include Genesis 17:8, perhaps recognizing that the covenant of God focuses less on the land and more on relationships with people. In fact, only one verse in this entire chapter mentions the gift of a geographical place. Quite apparently, what matters most to God is that there be a hope-filled, loving connection between God and humanity. Abraham and Sarah are expected to be good and faithful people, to "walk before (God) and be blameless" (17:1b). We have probably gotten into more conflicts on this planet over disputed lands and property rights than from any other issue. To this day ancient arguments continue with intensity over national boundaries. When will we learn that our covenant with God is primarily about loving people and not about owning property? It is about justice, peace, and unconditional love.

After God's meeting with Abram, Abram's life took on a radical new direction. He was no longer simply a wealthy owner of herds. He became God's chosen representative to be "the ancestor of a multitude of nations" (17:5b). His purpose was to be far more than accumulating wealth and seeking earthly security. He was asked to fulfill God's plan and to enable God's future to become reality. This divine election of Abraham and Sarah necessarily involved their moving forward with hopeful attitudes, embracing the possibilities that lay ahead and serving as witnesses or advocates for this new covenant. Notice that Sarah was to have a significant place in the development of the covenant. She was more than a bit player in this unfolding drama. The final two verses of our passage tell us of her central role: "I will bless her, and she shall give rise to nations; kings of peoples shall come from her" (17:16b).

In biblical times when new life or direction was given, God often gave new names to the persons involved. Perhaps it was a way of reminding the recipients of that special divine moment and of their ongoing responsibilities. To add emphasis to the momentousness of God's covenant with Abraham and Sarah, the writers of

Genesis also employ another name for God at this place in the text, *El Shaddai*, Hebrew for "God of the Mountains" or "God Almighty." Until now the Hebrews had largely been a nomadic people, a band of loosely connected wanderers. This new covenant with God, which included promises of a permanent home and deep roots, was designed to produce spiritual growth in the community and a richer, more complete understanding of God's nature.

What was true for our Hebrew ancestors applies to us as well, though we may consider ourselves to be more intellectually sophisticated. We have the benefit of centuries of profound theological reflection, yet we still do not comprehend the fullness of God's being. Should we not, therefore, unclench our minds and free ourselves from our limited, outmoded concepts in order to embrace God's fresh and creative revelations? For example, Christians in other cultures offer us a wealth of insights about God, provided we are willing to listen and learn.

Abraham and Sarah accepted change rather gracefully. Their understanding of God was reshaped; their relationship to God was shifted; their duties increased exponentially. They received new names, a new son, and new marching orders. This renewing, reviving power of God that entered Abraham and Sarah's lives is the very essence of our hope and the assurance of our future.

What pressures and problems do you face in your daily life that cause you to clench up and close down to God's loving presence? that make you resist the touch of other people?

What spiritual resources help you to stay open to God's grace and to retain an optimistic attitude toward life?

When changes occur, especially those that catch you by surprise, what insights might you learn from Abraham and Sarah about how to accept them?

PLUNGING INTO THE PROMISE
Romans 4:13-25

I appreciate the creative and thought-provoking biblical paraphrases of Eugene H. Peterson in *The Message*, for example, Romans 4:20: "He [Abraham] didn't tiptoe around God's promise asking cautiously skeptical questions. He plunged into the promise and came up strong, ready for God, sure that God would make good on what he had said."[2] Paul wanted his readers to understand that Abraham and Sarah grabbed hold firmly of God's promises and steadfastly moved forward to greet them. They did not concentrate on their failures, weaknesses, or advanced years. By faith they believed God, "being fully convinced that God was able to do what he had promised" (Romans 4:21).

When we believe in our own

human efforts, we are bound to be pessimists because by ourselves we accomplish so little; and even our greatest successes soon unravel. But when we believe and trust in God's grace, we are bound to be optimists because even our darkest moments and biggest failures are transformed by God into blessings. With faith in God, our hope is secure. We know, though the journey may be long and difficult, we will one day safely reach our ultimate destination. With this unwavering faith in our Creator, we are given courage to attempt tasks that seem humanly unattainable. The angel Gabriel put it succinctly when informing a youthful Mary that she had been chosen to bear God's Son: "For nothing," he told her, "will be impossible with God" (Luke 1:37).

The naysayers were out in force when a congregation's parish council voted to build a Habitat for Humanity house; to raise all the money and do all the work themselves; and to do the project's entire construction phase in a five-day "blitz build." "Can't be done," said an old carpenter. "A four-bedroom house like that will take months to build. The finish work alone will require several weeks." Others in the rural community nodded their heads in agreement.

"It took me half a year just to remodel my kitchen," a middle-aged lady said. "And I hired professionals to do most of the hard stuff."

"If God wants us to build this home, and goodness knows our town needs affordable housing, then we can do it." Heads turned because the speaker was a slim young woman, the president of the church's youth group. She spoke with conviction, with an authority far beyond her tender years. A number of people in attendance clapped. Her parents positively beamed. Several adults were embarrassed that God had had to strengthen their faith through the words of someone so young. Others remained skeptical. You could see from their faces that they did not much like a mere child telling them what to do, let alone quite possibly speaking for God.

The decision was made to proceed with the project. Fundraising events earned most of the money and also built a wonderful sense of fellowship. Skilled craftsmen and women signed on as volunteers. Businesses in the community caught the excitement and donated supplies. The usual problems and delays during construction arose; but at the end of five days, a solidly built, attractive house sat on what had once been a junk strewn, overgrown weed patch. When the family was handed the keys, there was not a dry eye anywhere. If nothing else, the project was worth the effort to see people working together, like a ten-year-old boy and a ninety-three-year-old great grandmother painting and laughing side by side. The congregation knew without a doubt that it was by faith that their Habitat house was completed in such a short time. They rejoiced as they shouted together a freely translated version of Psalm 127:1. "Truly the Lord has built this house, and those who built it did not labor in vain!"

The promise and power to do great deeds are gifts from God. Paul wrote, "For this reason it depends on faith, in order that the promise may rest on grace" (Romans 4:16). Life is not easy. It probably never has been. The promises of God to Abraham and Sarah, and those made to us as well, do not ignore the presence of pain, trouble, and injustice in the world. They rather provide us with an unshakable confidence, an unwavering hope, and an unquenchable faith.

Are you a toe-dabbling Christian or a jump-into-the-deep-end Christian? Which variety does God want us to be?

What motivates you to get out of bed in the morning—the alarm clock and the smell of breakfast or a desire to see what wonders and joys God has in store for you? Why?

In a time when it would be easy to yield to pessimism, in what concrete ways does faith keep you optimistic?

WINDOWS NOT MIRRORS
Mark 8:31-38

Once upon a time, so the story goes, a congregation removed all the windows of its church building and replaced them with mirrors. The recommendation came from the Beautification Committee. "Being able to see outside when we're worshiping is such a distraction," they said. "We gather to praise and glorify God, not to see poor children in our neighborhood playing in the street, homeless people wandering by, or even ambulances rushing on their way to the hospital." Heads nodded, and somebody suggested a solution: replace the clear glass with mirrors. After a brief discussion, the vote was unanimously in favor of the motion.

When the work was completed, the congregation was quite pleased with the results. It enabled them to appreciate the full beauty of their sanctuary: the wonderful grain of the oak pews, the rich highlights of the plush red carpet, and especially the polished brass of the huge cross that hung suspended above the altar. As an additional benefit, with but a glance they could admire their own Sunday finery, make certain their hair was perfectly in place, and secretly watch other parishioners to see who was not paying attention to the sermon or whose children were misbehaving. Perhaps best of all, no one outside could look inside and make them feel uncomfortable. The mirrors worked so well that they soon put them in all the Sunday school rooms, the fellowship hall, and the pastor's office.

In this Sunday's Gospel passage,

Peter is the disciple who might have preferred mirrors rather than windows. Jesus quite openly and honestly tells the Twelve that he must "undergo great suffering, and be rejected by the elders, the chief priests, and the scribes, and be killed, and after three days rise again" (Mark 8:31). It is not what Peter wants to hear. So Peter takes Jesus aside and rebukes him. He may have explained to Jesus that this was no way to run a successful religious operation; that he would not attract many followers letting himself suffer and be killed; and besides, as God's Son, he was supposed to be victorious, the One who wins the battle, not loses it.

Let's not be too quick to condemn Peter; to stick our noses in the air and say, "How could you, of all people, say something like this?" Remember, we have the blessing of living in post-Resurrection times. Peter did not. Plus we may not be quite as blunt or honest with Jesus as Peter was. Nevertheless, in our own subtle, indirect ways, we often communicate the same attitude. We are not always that convinced about the redemptive power of Christ's suffering, particularly if he expects us to suffer with him. We much prefer to skip over the pain of Good Friday and to go directly to Easter morning's joy.

Since time is short and events are happening quickly, Jesus does not tell a parable or offer a lengthy discourse. Instead, he immediately takes Peter aside and sets him straight. Peter, who rebuked Jesus, gets a full dose of that word's true meaning. Jesus' strong words are intended to produce radical change in Peter's heart and mind. I take consolation in the fact that Jesus did not say to Peter, "Go away," or "Get lost!" He rebuked him with this now famous phrase: "Get thee behind me, Satan!" (8:33, KJV). Jesus was not condemning Peter to everlasting damnation. He was correcting Peter's limited and inadequate concept of the Messiah. Peter, and perhaps the other disciples, too, did not expect Christ to suffer; and they certainly were not ready for him to die at the hands of his human opponents.

When we are honest with ourselves, most of us must admit we struggle intellectually over the same issue. Why did Jesus suffer? He calmed the storm, changed water into wine, fed multitudes with a child's sack lunch, healed the sick, and raised the dead; how could this worker of wonders and miracles allow his enemies to defeat him?

Mark quotes Jesus' explanation. First the Master addresses Peter: "You are setting your mind not on divine things but on human things" (8:33b). Peter apparently liked the taste of the sweet life, as we do; and I do not mean chocolate. We want a comfortable existence where things go well outwardly; where those we love prosper and succeed; where the church we attend grows, underwrites its budget, and has a big youth group. There is nothing wrong with this picture, except there are far more important things both in this life and the next. We are asked to give freely of ourselves and of our abundance in service to others, to be obedient to God's will, and to love people as God has loved us.

Then Jesus goes on to speak to the rest of the disciples and the crowd. No biblical scholar, no theologian, and certainly not this writer can possibly express these truths more effectively or powerfully. Read and savor the words of Jesus in Mark 8:34-35: "If any want to become my followers, let them deny themselves and take up their cross and follow me. For those who want to save their life will lose it, and those who lose their life for my sake, and for the sake of the gospel, will save it."

This lifestyle of giving yourself away for the sake of others is to be offered as a gift, not as a grudging duty or chore. We cannot delegate our ministry to someone else; nor can it be done with mirrors. We must take up our own cross and follow Christ. We must genuinely care about our neighbors. As disciples of Jesus Christ, we are to approach people with open arms rather than with clenched fists, to be vulnerable and accessible even when it is not convenient for us. As John Wesley said in a watch night service: "Christ has many services to be done; some are easy, others are difficult; some bring honor, others bring reproach; some are

suitable to our natural inclinations, and temporal interests, others are contrary to both. In some we may please Christ and please ourselves; in others we cannot please Christ except by denying ourselves. Yet the power to do all these things is assuredly given us in Christ, who strengthens us."[3]

For most of us this yielding of ourselves to God's purposes is done in small, quiet, and humble ways. Occasionally God presents us with a grand and glorious opportunity for service. But woe be it to those who sit and wait for such moments. They will miss the rewards of loving one another day by day. They will never know the joy of true servanthood. Sacrificing our self-interests, denying our personal desires, giving up some of our creature comforts are not the gravy of our Christian faith. They are the meat and potatoes, the heart and soul of the gospel.

Let's remember that the Roman and Jewish authorities did not take Jesus' life from him. He willingly gave it (John 10:18). In our own small way, may this be true of our lives as well. Obviously, we do not wish to be used, abused, and burned out. But we do want to give of ourselves freely and to unclench our lives as Christ unclenched his. May we allow others to know all of us, to experience the depth of our love, to share in the fullness of our joy and hope.

How can the church be successful in attracting new people, in building programs and attendance, and in raising needed funds, yet remain faithful to Jesus' call to deny ourselves and to serve humanity?

What does it mean to be in the world but not of the world (Mark 8:36)?

In what way has suffering been a positive, healing, even redemptive experience in your life?

What does it mean to set our minds on human things?

What might Jesus have included among "divine things" if he had made a list for Peter?

---

[1]From *Guerillas of Grace*, by Ted Loder (Innisfree Press, 1984); page 17.

[2]From *The Message*; page 312.

[3]From *The Book of Worship* (1964); page 387.

Channels of God's Grace

Scriptures for Lent:
The Third Sunday
Exodus 20:1-17
1 Corinthians 1:18-25
John 2:13-22

When I was a grade school youngster, my family lived on the edge of a small town in eastern Washington. A quarter mile below our house, across a cow pasture and through a meadow, was a beautifully pure stream. I spent many a pleasant summer afternoon playing by its banks. I sent tiny bark boats floating away on grand adventures, skipped rocks on the rare stretches of smooth water, and constructed rock dams. At least I tried. None of these creations was ever successfully completed since I always built where the creek bed was narrowest. It was there that the waters moved most quickly in their rush toward the mighty Columbia River. The stream almost seemed to giggle at my puny attempts. No matter how hard I labored, the water found a way to keep flowing on.

The same is true of God's grace. It flows into our lives in spite of our indifference, our complacence, and even our antagonism. Perhaps this is what John Wesley meant by prevenient grace; God is at work in our lives before we are aware of it, preparing us to receive sometime in the future the gift of salvation.

God's love has an infinite number of channels at its disposal. The Old Testament Law was a river of grace gushing over the Hebrew people, and nowhere more abundantly than in the Ten Commandments. Found in two places, Exodus 20 and Deuteronomy 5, the Decalogue was the source of ethical standards and set a framework for community building among a loosely knit band of wanderers. No set of laws has been more beloved through the centuries yet more frequently broken. They are like deep channels through which the grace of God flows, establishing the boundaries or limits that make possible our worship of God and our love for one another.

In 1 Corinthians 1, Paul boldly declares that the crucified and risen Christ is God's waterfall of grace under which we stand, by which we are absolutely drenched with love. To those who seek outward signs and strive after human wisdom, this idea will not make sense. But to those who by faith take the plunge through baptism, who jump in over their heads, it is rebirth and refreshment and joy. The cross of Christ is the source of our salvation.

In the Gospel passage for this Sunday, we discover how God reacts when those who should be helping this grace move freely into the lives of people instead hinder its flow. In John 2, Jesus acts decisively to remove the blockages. He enters the great Temple in Jerusalem at the busiest time of the year and causes quite a commotion. The moneychangers and Temple authorities no doubt considered his action bad for business. In God's eyes it was a necessary cleansing. Jesus was trying to remove the logjams erected by institutional religion in order to allow God's grace to flood the whole nation. After Jesus left, Temple employees probably cleaned up the place; and everybody went back to business as usual. Something was different, however. He who was greater than the Temple announced by his action that God had cut a new, incredibly deep and wide channel of grace. The world would never be the same again.

A LOVING AND LIBERATING GIFT
EXODUS 20:1-17

Jewish rabbis, in ancient times, placed a drop of honey on the tongues of their students whenever a verse from the Torah was successfully memorized. They wanted their young charges to experience the sweetness of the law rather than to think of it as restrictive, punitive, or a bitter pill to swallow. The honey was a way of saying that the first five books of the Bible, the Torah, are pleasant and good. They contain God's law as a divine gift and an everlasting blessing, a channel of God's grace.

Yet, the Ten Commandments have gotten bad press, according to J. Ellsworth Kalas. In his book *The Ten Commandments From the Back Side*, Kalas writes, "Someone has convinced us that God imposed these laws on us in order to keep us from enjoying life. Not at all! In fact, the ten commandments are the gift of a loving God. They are intended to make the road of life smoother, the journey less complicated, the destination more certain. As such, they may be our best friends."[1]

These laws, in fact, were the beginning of a revolutionary social experiment. This was to be no utopia. The laws are realistic to the point of bluntness. They form the moral foundation on which a community of faith was built and a great nation came into existence.

The revelation of these laws to Moses at Sinai was the continuation of God's process to set the people free. They had found release from slavery in Egypt. Now the theme, "Let my people go," finds a voice in these commandments. The Hebrews are given the means to live together peacefully in society by sharing a common focus and faith in one God and by having the possibility of healthy relationships among themselves. In all periods of history, nations and cities and even tiny villages have had boundaries. Since their inception, the Ten Commandments have set the spiritual and moral boundaries for Jewish and Christian communities.

God had much to say to Moses on that mountain. When God had finished the message, "he gave him the two tablets of the covenant, tablets of stone, written with the finger of God" (Exodus 31:18). The first four of those commandments address our relationship to God; the remaining six address our responsibilities to our neighbors. Together, however, they comprise a complete set, because the way we understand God fundamentally determines the way we treat one another.

The first commandment, "You shall have no other gods before me" (20:3), has to do with our ultimate loyalty. God states up front that our number one priority is God. Rather direct and to the point, wouldn't you say? The problem, of course, is that we are easily distracted. Human history has demonstrated over and over again how immense is our tendency to be led astray. We are able to resist this temptation by going back to basics, by returning regularly to square one—to God.

"You shall not make for yourself an idol.... You shall not bow down to them or worship them" (20:4-5). God cannot be domesticated. This God of the universe is not the private property of any person or group and cannot be located exclusively in any one denomination, nation, or other human institution. We cannot tame the glory, power, and majesty of God. We must avoid investing temporary things with ultimate meaning. Cheap imitations are exactly that.

Commandment number three is an admonition to hold our Creator in high regard: "You shall not make wrongful use of the name of the LORD your God" (20:7). This law is not just about cursing and profanity, although such disrespectful, hurtful behavior is surely included in the command. God's name possesses great power and mystery. It is never to be used lightly, carelessly, and certainly not profanely. Of course, our most prevalent wrongful use may be the failure to speak God's name often enough. We have a standing invitation to address God by name, to be personally acquainted with our Creator. It is indeed a high honor, one we should always respect. God's name is a name above all other names that we are to speak often and with loving affection.

In the days of my youth, I was not allowed to play cards or to go to movies on Sunday. The only businesses in town open on Sunday were one drugstore and one gas station. It was how society interpreted commandment number four in the mid-twentieth century. "Remember the sabbath day, and keep it holy" (20:8). The law points out that even God needed a day off following the hard work of creation. God is not a workaholic. The Creator paused on the seventh day to enjoy what had been accomplished, to bask in the wondrous beauty and promise of it all.

We who are created in God's image need a rhythm in our lives, too. Our human bodies and souls require times of refreshment and renewal. We need opportunities for family and community building, for rest and recovery. Even the soil needs to lie fallow for a season. Noise and constant activity crowd in on us. One day out of seven for quietness and reflection, for worship and sharing our lives, is not too much to expect of ourselves. The key is to "keep it holy," to converse and act in ways that draw us closer to God, closer to one another, and closer to creation.

Since the beginning of time, older generations have sought to pass their values on to younger ones. It has usually been a struggle. Even so, it is a challenge worth our best efforts. Temporary trends and passing fads do not matter. But the abiding truths contained in the Decalogue must not be lost. This is the intent of the fifth commandment: "Honor your father and your mother, so that your days may be long in the land that the LORD your God is giving you" (20:12). "To honor" literally means "to give weight to" and implies a two-way caring, a shared dignity between parents and their children.

The final five laws are tersely written: "You shall not murder" (20:13) is the sixth commandment. Viewed in a positive light, it calls us to value human life as a precious gift from God. It inspires us to have reverence for all life, to never use or abuse persons for selfish purposes, to live gently and peacefully on the earth.

"You shall not commit adultery" (20:14) is the seventh commandment. Its point is quite clear: We are not to misuse the beautiful yet fragile gift of intimacy. Human sexuality can be either an exquisite mystery or an extremely destructive urge. God expects us to use it as a blessing to help create profound and tender bonds of love.

I remember a time when we did not need to lock the doors of our houses, churches, and cars; when only banks had security systems; when vandalism was rare and graffiti virtually unknown. The eighth commandment speaks to these problems with four simple words: "You shall not steal" (20:15). We are not to take from or destroy what is precious to another person. This includes physical property and so much more: people's dignity and self-worth, their safety and freedom, even their joy and good humor. In an age when unfortunately many persons admit to shoplifting and cheating on their taxes, we would do well to teach this commandment emphatically to others and to rigorously practice it ourselves.

"You shall not bear false witness against your neighbor" (20:16). The ninth commandment is directed to individuals and to the judicial system. People are to be truth tellers: to be honest in business dealings, to avoid gossip, to be true to their word. Our legal system is to be an institution where truth is held sacred. Community is possible only when there is an arena of impartiality, where justice is applied equally to all persons.

The philosophy of "the grass is greener on the other side of the fence" may explain why we need to have the final commandment: "You shall not covet your neighbor's house...wife...slave...ox ...donkey, or anything that belongs to your neighbor" (20:17). We are to curb the intensity of our desire so as not to hurt others or to damage our relationships with them. When our wants are out of control, we not only adversely effect others, we make ourselves miserable as well.

In summary, the Ten Commandments reveal a God who is active in human affairs, who cares enough about the health of our relationships to say no, and who provides us with the resources we need to make wise decisions.

What are your earliest recollections of the Ten Commandments? Are these memories basically positive or negative for you?

Which two or three of these requirements would you emphasize if you were asked to produce a multi-million dollar national media campaign?

Under what circumstances is saying no more loving than saying yes?

GOD'S EXTRAORDINARY WAYS
1 Corinthians 1:18-25

The suffering and death of Jesus on the cross that Good Friday satisfied neither the Jewish people's desire for a sign nor the Greek's intellectual demands. Both groups tripped over the Crucifixion as a channel of God's grace and could not seem to aright themselves.

The Jews expected dramatic events to overwhelm them, to absolutely convince them beyond doubt that this was the Messiah. Before we raise our eyebrows at Paul's Jewish contemporaries, however, we would be well-advised to examine our own hearts and minds. Our prayerful conversation might go something like this: "O God, don't make me struggle with questions and doubt. I'm tired of seeking answers and searching for your will. Give me a sign. Something visible, something even I can't miss. I want a snap-of-my-fingers faith." The answer comes gently yet firmly. "My child, you remember, don't you, that I'm the One who spoke to the prophet Elijah? He thought I'd speak through the wind, earthquake, or fire. I chose instead the sound of sheer silence. Or tell me, child, how did I announce the forthcoming birth of my Son? Was it not with starlight radiating in the quiet night sky, with the rustle of angel wings, with the lowing of cattle? Read again from my Word where it says, 'Let anyone who has an ear listen to what the Spirit is saying'" (Revelation 3:13).

Then there were the Greeks who considered this crucifixion/ resurrection business to be utter foolishness. In their opinion, divine beings were so far removed from earthly matters that they would never stoop to us, never come in human form, let alone suffer and die on a cross. Unthinkable! To the Greek mind, the gods were totally apathetic to the humble affairs of mere mortals. The cross of Christ simply did not fit into any of their intellectual boxes. They were more impressed by spellbinding orators and persuasive debaters. Wise people were called sophists; that is, sophisticated and clever in ways of the world.

What a surprise there is for persons like the Greeks who adhere to a radically transcendent theology. They may be amazed to discover that God's Son sat on the ground to play with children, spat in the dust to make a mud plaster and place it on the eyes of a man who was blind, knelt down to wash his disciples' feet, broke bread, ate with sinners, and touched the sick and unclean.

But hold on. We are not done yet with this nonsense. Paul has the audacity to claim that the best method or channel of God's grace, of inspiring people to accept this gift of salvation, is preaching: common, often not very entertaining, sometimes too long, and occasionally sprinkled with split infinitives and dangling participles. Paul is talking about sermons from the heart; honest and solid proclamations of Christ crucified and risen, witnessing to the power and glory of God's amazing grace.

The Message captures the essence of this claim: "Since the world in all its fancy wisdom never had a clue when it came to knowing God, God in his wisdom took delight in using what the world considered dumb—preaching, of all things!—to bring those who trust him into the way of salvation" (1 Corinthians 1:21).[2]

When you are honest with yourself, does the cross of Christ pose a bit of a stumbling block for you? Why or why not?

What about human nature makes you susceptible to fast-talking, glib-tongued orators?

What are the essential qualities of a truly inspiring and effective sermon?

SOMETHING GREATER THAN THE TEMPLE
John 2:13-22

How would you react if someone came into your Sunday morning worship service and noisily, abruptly brought it to a halt? Dumped the offering plates on the floor, and kicked the checks and money all around? Scattered the hymnals, ripped up the preacher's notes, knocked over the baptismal font, and tossed the choir's folders out the window? And did all this on Easter morning? You would then have a good idea how the Temple priests and moneychangers felt on that day when Jesus strode into the outer courtyard with fire in his eyes.

Jesus had been with his disciples and family in Cana of Galilee at a wedding celebration. Afterward they stopped for a few days in Capernaum, then proceeded to Jerusalem. It was the city's busiest time of the year. It may seem incredible, but more than two million Jewish pilgrims sometimes were packed into the Holy City during the Passover celebration. It must have been controlled chaos in the Temple, especially in the outer court of the Gentiles. The moneychangers were hard at work, exchanging foreign and therefore unclean currency for Jewish coins or Temple monies. Both the annual Temple tax and the purchase of sacrificial animals required religiously "clean" money,

for which there was a fairly steep rate of exchange and a hefty service charge.

Crowded there were sojourners, tired and perhaps poor from their travel expenses, being charged exorbitant fees. The practice was clearly unjust and was possibly outright extortion. Jesus had almost certainly known about this money-changing for years. His time now was short, however; so like the prophets of old, he made a dramatic entrance. First he got their attention by using a whip of cords to chase the sheep and cattle out. Then he poured out the coins, overturned the tables, and told those who sold doves, "Take these things out of here! Stop making my Father's house a marketplace!" (John 2:15-16).

Jesus once got into a heated discussion with some Pharisees concerning sabbath law. It seems he and his disciples were hungry and while walking through a field on the sabbath had plucked and eaten heads of grain. The Pharisees were aghast. Jesus must have sighed at their narrow literalism, then explained, "I tell you, something greater than the temple is here" (Matthew 12:6). The Savior of the world was in their midst, and they did not realize it. A love far greater than any they could image was now being channeled into the whole world. A wisdom far superior to any other was now available even to the humblest of people. But the Temple staff continued operating their elaborate sacrificial system rather than inviting worshipers to receive clean hearts and new and right spirits within. The Temple was all an outward show of piety. Plus it was apparently quite lucrative.

Our Gospel passage for this third Sunday in Lent serves as a helpful antidote to the tendency to become set in our ways, to go through the motions of our faith, and to forget our responsibility to welcome and accept strangers. The leaders of Jesus' day did not intentionally decide to lose the inner spark and spontaneity of their faith. It happened gradually. Perhaps they did not notice how exclusive and inhospitable they had become. The outer Court of the Gentiles, for example, was as far as non-Jews could proceed in the Temple. It was certainly no place for prayer and praise. Money was changing hands rather than hearts being touched.

If there are things in our congregations today that hold newcomers at arm's length, that keep them on the fringes, let us remember Jesus' hot anger directed toward those who made it nearly impossible for seekers to experience God's presence. Let this passage be a warning for us to never turn our churches into closed clubs where status is more prized than spirituality, where new people and fresh ideas are barely tolerated if not completely ignored, where we construct a blockade to the flow of God's grace rather than an open channel.

Jesus might have escaped unscathed had his Temple foray ended at this point in the proceedings. It did not. The Jewish leaders, understandably upset and a bit cranky, demanded that Jesus justify his drastic actions: "What sign can you show us for doing this?" (John 2:18). Jesus' reply was certainly not what they had anticipated. He suggested that if the Temple were destroyed, he would raise it again in three days. "Three days?" they exclaimed. "We've been working on this building complex for forty-six years, and you're going to rebuild it in three days? Surely you jest." Jesus was not laughing. He was serious, although he was referring not to the Temple structure but to his own body.

Something far greater than the magnificent Temple edifice was present there, Jesus the Christ. Yet few people realized it. They were too involved in keeping their own schedules and following their own small agendas. Jesus' prophetic words about the Temple's destruction did eventually come to pass. Roman troops leveled it to the ground in A.D. 70. Yet, that was not what Jesus was trying to communicate. He was sharing the same message he later delivered to the Samaritan woman at the well: "The hour is coming, and is now here, when the true worshipers will worship the Father in spirit and truth, . . . God is spirit, and those who worship him must worship in spirit and truth" (4:23-24).

The cleansing of the courtyard

and the mere mention that the entire Temple could be destroyed most assuredly hastened Jesus' arrest and death. Yet his every word was true, and his motives were pure and loving. Something far greater than the Temple, magnificent though it was, had come into the world. The Word of God, the perfect channel of God's grace, had become incarnate, had chosen to live among us as a kind and gentle person, Jesus of Nazareth.

This potent lesson from Jesus as told by John contains a truth we ignore at great peril. The prolific Scottish biblical interpreter, William Barclay, put it this way: "Our contact with God, our entry into his presence, or our approach to him is not dependent on anything [human] hands can build or [human] minds devise. In the street, in the home, at business, on the hills, on the open road, in church we have our inner temple, the presence of the Risen Christ forever with us throughout all the world."[3] What wonderful tidings of hope!

How long does it take newcomers in your congregation to be granted access to the innermost circles of fellowship and leadership? If your answer is more than several months, why does it take this amount of time?

In what ways could you become more welcoming to strangers and to new ideas?

In what ways are you serving as a channel of God's grace?

---

[1]From *The Ten Commandments From the Back Side*, by J. Ellsworth Kalas (Abingdon Press, 1998); page 19.

[2]From *The Message*; page 339.

[3]From *The Daily Bible Study Series: The Gospel of John, Vol. 1* (The Westminster Press, 1975); page 117.

From Wilderness to Eternity

Scriptures for Lent:
The Fourth Sunday
Numbers 21:4-9
Ephesians 2:1-10
John 3:14-21

Years ago, when our six children were all at home, we rented a large motor home for our summer vacation and went to Washington, DC, some three thousand miles across the country. The trip was quite an adventure. We enjoyed seeing a number of our country's greatest attractions: Yellowstone Park, Mount Rushmore, the historical sites in and around Boston. By the time we arrived in our nation's capital, we were tired. Nevertheless, we tried to see it all. The weather was hot and humid; our motor home did not have air conditioning; and our teen-age family members had reached their limit of togetherness. I recall the argument we had on the marble steps of a Smithsonian building as if it were yesterday. One son was ready to walk home to the Pacific Northwest rather than spend another minute with his siblings. To make matters worse, we later got trapped inside the vehicle when rough roadway loosened bolts on the door handle. We finally lowered the youngest and smallest child out a window to go for help.

Our family certainly learned first-hand a lot of geography and history of these United States that summer; but like Moses in the wilderness, we also heard a great deal of grumbling, muttering, and murmuring. We got the usual complaints: bathrooms too dirty to use, six pages of menu from which to choose and nothing for them to eat, no television or video games to watch, a brother or sister sitting in their special spot, and on and on. By the grace of God, we made it back home a month and eight thousand miles later, still speaking to one another and still in love. In fact, we were more closely bonded as a family. We had gotten to know one another up close and intimately. We had shared a long and difficult journey together, but it proved to be a defining moment for our family unit and blessed us with a lifetime of wonderful memories.

The travels of the Hebrew people from slavery in Egypt into the Promised Land were far longer, exceedingly more arduous, and the stakes were the highest possible—a matter of survival. It is no wonder, then, that their charismatic leader, Moses, soon became the target of people's anxieties and complaints. It is rather amazing that in those forty years of struggle there were not more moans and groans. God was with the Hebrews every step of the way, providing for their necessities, giving strong discipline and welcomed assurance as they prepared to enter their new homeland.

In Ephesians, Paul writes of a different sort of journey, a spiritual movement from following the course of this world to being made alive in Christ. Again, it can be a struggle for us to make such a journey. We fast-food generations crave instant gratification and immediate results, plus we expect comfortable accommodations along the way. But the journey from death to life, from sin to salvation, is not something we can take by ourselves, instantly. It is "by grace you have been saved through faith, and this is not of your own doing; it is the gift of God" (Ephesians 2:8). Since it is a gift, God wraps and offers it to us as God sees fit. We do not call the shots. The timetable is God's alone. Thankfully, we do not ever walk alone. God is our faithful companion on the journey.

This faith journey is described in the Gospel of John as having an eternal dimension. God came in Jesus not to condemn the world, not to punish, but to affirm us. The gift of God's grace is not a one-time offer. It is available to everyone everywhere. God's love does not come with a limited warranty. It is our source of hope forever.

ARE WE THERE YET, GOD?
Numbers 21:4-9

I believe *steamed* is the correct word. Or maybe *fuming, irate,* or *ticked off.* She was terribly upset because she could not find her choir robe. "Who took my robe?" she asked accusingly. "I left it on this hanger after practice, and now it's gone. It has my nametag on the collar, and I want it back immediately! Or else!" I decided it was the better part of wisdom not to ask what the "or else" might be. It was an obviously tense moment and not good timing since Sunday worship was about to begin. It seemed to me to be a major overreaction. Several other robes in her size were available. Anyway, by comparison to the troubles in the world at that moment, this was the tiniest of inconveniences. Half a million refugees in the Balkans were struggling for life. Families were being torn apart. Thousands of innocent people were being systematically slaughtered. Yet, there we were in our comfortable and safe church building murmuring about a missing choir robe.

This human problem is apparently age-old. The Hebrews had been freed by God from the degradations of slavery in Egypt. God had called Moses and Aaron to lead them safely on their journey. When they were thirsty, God provided water from a rock; when they were hungry, God sent manna from heaven. When they grew weary of a steady diet of that bland manna and wanted meat, God provided quail. The birds fell beside the camp about three feet deep. Now that is what I call being taken care of. About the only thing God did not do was clean, pluck, and cook the quail. Yet some of the people continued to murmur.

The word *murmur* is very communicative. It speaks of a quiet resentment, of muttering under one's breath, of whimpering and whining. Individuals who murmur could not possibly be pleasant traveling companions. They would be even more difficult to lead. We are told that "the people became impatient on the way" (Numbers 21:4b). It reminds me of taking children on a trip who, when barely out of the city limits, start asking, "Are we there yet?" They often continue their litany of murmuring the rest of the way non-stop.

Let's agree, however, that this forty-year sojourn was no picnic. The people escaped from Egypt with little more than the clothes on their backs. You remember how they did not even have time to let yeast rise and thus had to eat unleavened bread. The land across which they traveled was and still is mostly inhospitable, which may be an understatement. In addition, the original travelers had been slaves. They may have had their basic physical needs met, but they knew nothing of freedom. They had had little experience in making their own decisions. Their owners had likely kept them separated from one another; they would have been novices at community building. There were no travel brochures with glossy color photos of a plush tour or depicting the wonders of their final destination. The wilderness experiences of life are never easy. To their great credit, murmuring or not, the Israelites kept going. This was truly a journey of hope and trust and faith.

In our day, the wildernesses most of us must endure, at least in first world nations, do not involve this kind of physical deprivation. Our desert sojourns tend to be mental, emotional, and spiritual in nature. We struggle with anxiety and depression, with doubt and fear, with loneliness and hopelessness. We grumble about small and insignificant matters as well. Yet although we live thirty-five hundred years later than our ancient Hebrew sisters and brothers, give or take several hundred, we share a common trait. We too are accomplished murmurers. Students gripe about teachers and tests and having to get up in the morning. Adults complain about bosses, about working too hard and getting paid too little. Children grumble about their parents' discipline; the electorate mumbles about their political leaders; we all murmur about paying taxes.

Sometimes when the problems seem overwhelming, we pick even more at small things. My mother suffered painfully from the ravages of osteoporosis. Normally a sweet, uncomplaining person, she got cranky when someone tied her shoelaces with the bows too long. Her world seemed out of control. The future appeared to hold few blessings and little hope for her. So she muttered about tiny and seemingly unimportant things. The real issue, of course, was that she was facing a crisis of faith. Though she was a woman of profound courage and belief, she struggled to understand how such pain could possibly fit into God's plan for her life.

So also must it have been for those ancient wanderers in the Sinai Peninsula. What point was there in having a prolonged theological debate over the omnipotence or omniscience of God? Theirs was an uncertain future. There were no maps, no guarantees of success, not even the knowledge of whether there would be enough food for their children's next meal. Into this mix of anxious and troubled souls, God came in a surprising way: "Then the LORD sent poisonous serpents among the people, and they bit the people, so that many Israelites died" (21:6).

It is hard to know exactly what to make of this frightening event. It cannot be that God was deliberately hurting and destroying the very people that were so carefully brought out of Egypt. Perhaps these snakes were like seraphs, divine messengers of discipline. God's motive was surely to restore the Israelites' hope and trust. It forcefully demonstrated God's presence and authority in their midst.

The people repented of their sin, of speaking against God and against God's chosen leader, Moses. Moses went to bat for them. He served as their advocate before God. The antidote to their plight was to make a bronze serpent and to place it on a pole. Anyone who looked at it would be restored to health and life. It caused the people to stop looking down at their scuff marks in the sand and to lift up their eyes, to focus their attention, hope, and trust on the God who loved them. The bronze serpent was a vivid reminder that they would never be alone, that their hope was in God.

What were the basic or underlying causes for the Israelite's murmuring?

What makes you grumble and mutter to yourself?

Does murmuring ever serve a useful purpose? Why or why not?

Have you had any "wilderness wanderings" in your life? What caused them? How long did they last?

What resources enabled you to find your "promised land"?

GOD'S WORK OF ART
Ephesians 2:1-10

Paul had a way with words, didn't he? Our lection for this fourth Sunday in Lent reads like the lyrics to a beautiful song. These verses from Ephesians form an exquisite hymn to God's mercy and grace. Paul is not providing a precise theological definition of salvation by faith. He is pouring out his heart. He is singing a love song to God. Listen to this lilting phrase: "We are God's work of art, created in Christ Jesus to live the good life as from the beginning he meant us to live it" (Ephesians 2:10, *The New Jerusalem Bible*). We are God's work of art, a priceless masterpiece of our Creator.

I recently had the privilege of observing the baptisms of several adults. Before each knelt to receive the sacramental water, he or she stood in front of the congregation and spoke these words: "I am beloved, a precious child of God and beautiful to behold." The voices of several of them choked with emotion; and I noticed more than a few tears being shed in the pews, including my own. The baptismal candidates could have added this adaptation of Paul's words, "I am God's work of art."

Paul did not wear rose-colored glasses when he penned these words. He had a realistic estimate of humanity's condition when left to its own devices. He talks of how we once lived in the passions of our flesh and followed the desires of our lower nature. Understanding Paul's concept of sin is important and enlightening. Sin is not primarily defined in his writings as a list of immoral behaviors such as stealing, lying, adultery, and the like. Paul, of course, condemns such practices. Here in Ephesians, however, he is looking at the big picture of sin and defines it as a failure to hit the target. It is our falling short of what God intends us to be. Sin is our unwillingness to risk striving after our highest potential and to not accept the gifts God wants to give to each of us.

This definition of sin applies to the entire human race. We may not be guilty of committing specific sinful acts, but "all have sinned and fall short of the glory of God" (Romans 3:23). Matthew Fox, a Dominican scholar and theologian, says that sin is a lack of imagination, of failing to employ our creative energies, of limiting the joy of life. "By sinning in this way we refuse to fall in love with life, to love what is lovable, to savor life's simple and non-elitist pleasures, to befriend pleasure, to celebrate the blessings of life, to return thanks for such blessings by still more blessing."[1]

Though Paul may have had his imperfections, loving and celebrating the blessings of life certainly were not among them. I recommend reading and rereading Ephesians 2:4-10 until it literally seeps through your pores. Listen to a portion of this scriptural rhapsody as translated into contemporary English by Eugene Peterson: "It's a wonder God didn't lose his temper and do away with the whole lot of us. Instead, immense in mercy and with an incredible love, he embraced us. He took our sin-dead lives and made us alive in Christ. Now God has us where he wants us, with all the time in this world and the next to shower grace and kindness upon us in Christ Jesus."[2]

A pastor friend of mine has a favorite and frequently used saying whenever things happen serendipitously. When, in spite of our human frailties, everything works out perfectly, she joyfully exclaims, "It's a 'God Thing!' " She is right. Paul makes it crystal clear that God's grace is not something we deserve or earn. It does not happen as a result of our best planning or because of our list-making abilities. Salvation is not a paycheck for good works done. It is a free gift. "Saving is all his idea, and all his work. All we do is trust him enough to let him do it. It's God's gift from start to finish."[3]

If anybody in the history of the Christian faith ever earned the right to brag, to take credit for his many accomplishments, or to murmur when troubles came, it was surely Paul. Yet he never did. He came close when he was frustrated with the folks in the Corinthian church, a congregation that was being led astray from the basics of Jesus' teachings. So he offered his impressive credentials of suffering to prove his mettle. He listed his imprisonments, his floggings, a stoning, three shipwrecks, as well as various dangers, toils, and hardships (2 Corinthians 11:16-33). Instead of harping on his problems and difficulties, however, Paul sang God's praises, gloried in God's goodness and mercy, and found hope and delight in God's amazing grace.

What parallels might be made between the ways in which people are God's work of art and the greatest artistic efforts in human fields such as music, poetry, drama, sculpture, and painting?

Is it refreshing for you or frustrating to have sin defined as the failure to seek one's highest potential and to savor life's simple pleasures?

When has something wonderful happened that was not of your own doing, when you could have exclaimed, "It's a God thing!"?

GOD'S EXTRAVAGANT DIMENSIONS OF LOVE
John 3:14-21

An apocryphal story about the apostle John as an old man tells of his being invited frequently to preach in various congregations. When the sermon time came, he would slowly sit down on a chair provided for him, look out on the assembly of Christians, and then speak but one word: "Love." That's all John needed to say. His whole life and the entire body of his writings centered on that greatest of all gifts, love.

John 3:16, one of John's statements about love (see also 1 John 4:7), is surely among the most well-known and beloved verses in the Bible. In some ways it may be too familiar. It shows up on hand-painted signs being waved in the end zones at football games and behind home plate at the World Series. It's everywhere—stenciled on T-shirts, plastered on bill-boards, painted on the sides of buses. The surprising power and radical nature of these words may get lost in the shuffle.

Jesus first shared these now-famous words as part of a secretive nighttime visit with Nicodemus. He had just told this leader of the Jews that "no one can see the kingdom of God without being born from above" (John 3:3). Nicodemus came to Jesus with words of flattery and ended up having his faith shaken to its very roots. There may have been more dialogue in this meeting between the two men than we read in John's Gospel, but it seems clear that Jesus took the initiative. He had a major message to convey, not only to Nicodemus and the Jewish community, but to all persons for all time.

Perhaps to help Nicodemus, who was well-versed in the Hebrew Scriptures, grasp the radically new and profound nature of these words, Jesus noted how Moses lifted up the serpent in the wilderness. The Israelites were healed from poisonous snakebites simply by gazing on that bronze replica. Even so, said Jesus, "The Son of Man [must] be lifted up, that whoever believes in him may have eternal life" (3:14-15). With Jesus, the stakes are considerably higher than in the time of Moses. During the Exodus, the healings were limited in time and space. The bronze snake brought a much welcomed but outward and temporary solution to a specific problem. What Jesus offered in this new covenant was everlasting health, wholeness, and peace to the entire universe forever.

This was a mind-boggling idea, especially to a Jewish leader who considered his nation, among those in all the world, to have been chosen exclusively by God. Nicodemus was probably convinced there were boundaries to consider and conditions to be met, even for God's love. Jesus did not debate the point. He ignored it altogether. God's love, he explained to a flustered and bewildered Nicodemus, has no boundaries whatsoever, no limitations, no hidden agendas.

A number of years ago, I returned to school in a Doctor of Ministry program. The New Testament professor at San Francisco Theological Seminary was Dr. Herman Waetjen. We studied the

Gospel of John that summer, and every morning he brought to class his well-worn Greek New Testament. When he got to John 3:16, the good doctor's eyes lighted up. The English translation, "world," he explained, is from the Greek word *kosmos*, the source of the English word *cosmos*. The boundaries of God's grace and love are drawn wide indeed. In fact, God's loving kindness includes everyone and everything for all time and eternity. What a comforting and yet humbling thought. We who walk on the crust of a small blue sphere in a second-rate solar system of a minor galaxy are unconditionally loved by the God of the universe.

Paul put it as eloquently as humanly possible: "And I ask him [Christ] that with both feet planted firmly on love, you'll be able to take in with all Christians the extravagant dimensions of Christ's love. Reach out and experience the breadth! Test its length! Plumb the depths! Rise to the heights!"[4] Physicists have long searched for the single unifying principle of the universe, for some mysterious particle that holds it all together, for some unknown force to make sense of everything. I suggest that scientists have been looking in the wrong places. This unifying quality is not mechanical and physical; it is inward and spiritual. It has been with us since the Incarnation, ever since "the Word became flesh and lived among us" (John 1:14).

Love is the connective tissue of the cosmos. A statement of faith is needed to express it, not a mathematical formula. As Paul wrote, "In [Christ] all things in heaven and on earth were created, things visible and invisible, ... He himself is before all things, and in him all things hold together" (Colossians 1:16-17). God's love in Jesus Christ keeps us as individuals from coming apart, continuously seeks to bring unity to our human race, and in fact is the power that sustains an ever-expanding universe.

This love of God that dominates the Fourth Gospel is for John a "both/and" reality. That is, the fullness of love awaits us in eternity, yet is available in each and every moment of our lives right now. Because of the cross of Christ, eternal life is no longer restricted to the future but is also affirmed and experienced in our daily struggles. In our present earthbound condition, you and I are loved; we are accepted; we are not alone. God is with us: Emmanuel! We anticipate untold joys ahead. But God's love is not only "in the sweet by and by," it is with us in the wonderful here and now.

I myself experience hints of heaven when I am with our grandchildren. Nothing can compare with a two-year-old grandchild running full speed across a room to tackle grandpa with a loving hug around the knees or for that matter flying kites together in the park during a brisk spring breeze, holding hands while skipping down the sidewalk, watching a butterfly flit from blossom to blossom, reading Dr. Seuss with the book in one hand and a giggling child in my other arm, or saying our prayers together. Eternity begins right now. Thanks be to God!

Since we are created in God's image, it is an inescapable conclusion that we should love others as God loves us. We are to live in love's light, to embrace and nurture the beauty in all God's children, to affirm the precious gift of life in its every form. If God knows each of our thoughts and motives, yet does not condemn us, how dare we stand in judgment or condemnation of any other human being? We are created to love without conditions or boundaries, to accept one another as God in Christ has accepted us. "For God so loved the world that he gave his only Son" (John 3:16). God did not make an introductory deal, did not lease or lend his Son to us for a limited time, does not have a fifty thousand mile or five-year guarantee. This offer is good for everlasting love and eternal life.

What are some of the boundaries you draw around your relationships? In what ways do you try to restrict the free flow of God's love?

When has Christ literally held your life or that of your loved ones together?

If eternity is not only a future reality but begins right here and now, what changes might we make in our churches and society in order to reflect this truth?

What "hints of heaven" or "glimpses of eternity" do you have in your life?

---

[1]From *Original Blessing*, by Matthew Fox (Bear & Company, 1983); page 119.

[2]From *The Message*; page 403.

[3]From *The Message*; page 403.

[4]From *The Message*; page 405.

Behold, I Make All Things New

Scriptures for Lent:
The Fifth Sunday
Jeremiah 31:31-34
Hebrews 5:5-10
John 12:20-33

In the Revelation to John, a vision is given of a new heaven and a new earth, a blessed time when all tears will be wiped away from our eyes and death will be no more. This vision includes a voice like thunder coming from heaven's place of highest honor: "The one who was seated on the throne said, 'See, I am making all things new'" (Revelation 21:5). In the Northern Hemisphere the season of spring roughly coincides with our Christian season of Lent. Both represent times of new life and growth. In spring buds burst forth, bulbs break open, crocuses and daffodils bloom, and birds sing for joy. Lent is the equivalent of springtime for the soul. As the light of each succeeding day lengthens, so should the breadth and depth of our faith. As the air and earth gradually warm, so should our love for God and for our sisters and brothers. As creation clothes itself in beauty, so should our inner lives be radiant in glory.

Newness of life is one of the Bible's great themes. From the Genesis account of creation to the last chapters of Revelation, God finds innovative approaches to working with and expressing love for us upright walking, two-legged creatures. The three lectionary passages for this fifth Sunday in Lent are dramatic illustrations of God's fresh and novel methods. People of faith ought never to become complacent in their relationship with God. Just when we think we have figured out the Almighty One of the Universe, God comes to us in some unexpected way. God obviously enjoys surprises and uses them to keep us spiritually awake.

Out of the blue, the prophet Jeremiah presented a fundamental change in how the Israelites were to understand their covenant with God. No longer was it to be seen as distant from them. The covenant was to be as close as the beating of their hearts. The Law would not simply be carved on tablets of stone; it would be written within them. There would be an intimate and personal bond between the people and God.

Jeremiah 31 is thrilling and quite touching. In the midst of war's chaos and the pain of the Babylonian captivity, here are tidings of great hope. Through the decades of suffering that followed, the Israelites must have held tightly to these gracious and tender words. Yet sometimes we are not quite ready to receive and participate in God's new ways. Some Israelites in Jeremiah's day resisted his God-given message of truth. Many of us today similarly are not ready to experience this God who acts in surprising ways. We keep looking to the old forms of worship and miss the Spirit's presence in contemporary expressions. We are too caught up in oiling our religious machinery to notice the joyful freedom God wants to give us.

The author of the Letter to the Hebrews shares a unique perspective on Christ's role in our lives. The focus is on God's Son Jesus Christ, who is truly in touch with our lives, knows who we are and what we need, speaks our language, and through it all loves us dearly. In this Sunday's passage the writer says plainly that Jesus is the one we need. He is the "pioneer and perfecter of our faith" (Hebrews 12:2). He is our High Priest, who through his suffering and powerful praying connects us anew to the Source of Life. The answers to our searchings are not found in religious gimmicks or in passing fads. Neither should we place our trust in the latest self-help trends. Outward church trappings will not satisfy our deepest yearnings. Turn to Christ, the One appointed by God to be the source of our eternal salvation.

The Gospel passage is part of a sequence of truly amazing events in Jesus' life. In John 11, onlookers are absolutely astonished by the raising of Lazarus from the tomb. At least one disciple, Judas, is scandalized immediately thereafter when Mary anoints Jesus' feet with costly perfume (John 12:1-8). The following day a great throng welcomes Jesus with palm branches as he enters Jerusalem.

During the Passover festival, some Greeks approach Philip and ask if they might visit Jesus with the possible intention of following him. When Philip and Andrew ask Jesus if he wants to see these Gentiles, he does not just say, "Of course I do." He replies rather cryptically that the time of his glorification is near and that unless a grain of wheat dies it will never bear fruit. The disciples must have wondered, "Did he say yes or no?" Later they would come to understand what he meant, as Saint Francis did in the thirteenth century, "It is in dying that we are born to eternal life."

We who are just embarking on the twenty-first century have the luxury of having been exposed to this message countless times. Yet we still struggle with its shocking content and with the hope and newness of life Jesus' words bring to our lives.

A DIAMOND IN THE ROUGH
Jeremiah 31:31-34

The only place in the Old Testament where the words *new* and *covenant* are yoked together is here in Jeremiah 31. It is surprising to find a message of such hope in the midst of such incredible pain. Jeremiah had been predicting dire consequences for years. The people's faithlessness would surely result in God's severest discipline: poverty, famine, even captivity and exile. Ever since he had felt God's call to prophecy in 626 B.C., Jeremiah had been warning the nation to mend its ways and to return to the Lord. They had grown spiritually complacent and no longer placed their trust in God. Jeremiah held them accountable for their infidelity and forcefully called them to repent.

When the moment of disaster actually came in 587 B.C., when the mighty Babylonians destroyed Jerusalem and carried into exile all able-bodied Israelites, however, Jeremiah offered comforting words. He could have said, "I told you so"; but he did not. Compassion filled his heart for his suffering compatriots: "He who scattered Israel will gather him, and will keep him as a shepherd a flock" (Jeremiah 31:10b). The prophet proclaimed that though the Babylonians were temporarily victorious, God's covenant with Israel would last forever. Not even the greatest power in the world could alter that divine/human relationship. In the midst of utter tragedy, Jeremiah offered a lively hope with the promise of a glorious future.

Jeremiah's message in Chapter 31, verses 31-34 is one of the most beautifully profound and totally unexpected passages in the entire Bible. These verses are like a diamond in the rough, a jewel of hope set in the incomprehensible pain and sorrow of the nearly fifty year Babylonian Exile. They form one of the highest mountain peaks in Old Testament literature.

The words are surprising in part because Jeremiah was none too popular among his own people. They grew weary of his messages of doom and gloom. He was especially unwelcome to the rich, powerful, and famous. Having him hang around was bad for business. The King of Judah, Jehoiakim, had Jeremiah's prophecies read while he sat in front of a fireplace. After the reading of every three or four columns, the king used his penknife to slice off chunks of the scroll before throwing them into the fire (Jeremiah 36:20-23). God and Jeremiah, however, got the last word. With his secretary Baruch's help, Jeremiah once again dictated the first thirty-six chapters, then added sixteen more for good measure.

The new covenant shared by Jeremiah was not like the old one. What was primarily a binding commitment between God and the nation now had an added personal dimension. This new relationship included the individual and his or her responsibility. The law was not simply carved on stone tablets; now it was written in the hearts of men and women. This was no superficial change that Jeremiah prophesied. It was deep and permanent, offering dramatically new promises of personal wholeness and joy.

When God's laws are etched in rock, it is not difficult to ignore them, to walk away saying, "Those have nothing to do with me." It is the same reasoning we use when we fudge a bit on the speed limit and grumble about all the governmental regulations and red tape. When laws are external, we obey them because we are told we must. There will be serious consequences if we do not. We may comply, but we do not have to be happy about it.

Ah, but place that same law of love in someone's soul; and the motivation to accept and follow it comes from within. The old formally written contracts give way to the desires of the heart. Under this new covenant, lectures and scolding are unnecessary. Fire and brimstone preaching and motivation by guilt are out of place. These verses in Jeremiah 31 are not only solid theology, they are good educational theory as well. In fact, societies function best when "ought-to's" are kept to a minimum and "want-to's" are the order of the day.

More than five centuries would pass before Jeremiah's vision of a new covenant would finally become reality in Jesus. When that time came, Jeremiah knew there would be no need to teach others about God. We would all know God from the youngest of us to the oldest. Experiencing God's presence would be as natural as our breathing and the beating of our hearts.

The complete fulfillment of this gracious promise has not yet happened. As we await its fruition, let us frequently remind one another of God's wondrous love, correct one another's errors with compassion and kindness, teach and inspire, laugh and cry, hold hands and hug others on this shared journey of faith.

In what ways might it have been difficult for Jeremiah to switch gears quickly from prophesying dire consequences to proclaiming a lively hope and a wonderful future?

How might things change between employers and employees, teachers and students, parents and children, pastors and congregations, if we truly had God's word written on our hearts?

What "diamonds in the rough," what new sources of promise, do you see in the church today?

Where do you observe rays of hope in the contemporary world, including the perpetual trouble spots with their seemingly overwhelming problems?

OUR SOURCE OF ETERNAL SALVATION
Hebrews 5:5-10

As the old joke goes, the perfect pastor is a youthful thirty years old with twenty-five years of experience, works ninety hours a week yet has ample amounts of family time, wears the latest fashions, drives a fancy car, does it all on minimum salary with no charge cards, is slim and trim yet eats large helpings of everyone's famous recipes at potlucks. This discussion of what makes a wonderful minister has apparently been going on since the first century, except the writer of Hebrews offered a much more solid and adequate definition. In the opening four verses of Chapter 5, we discover the qualifications of an effective priest are: (1) to serve as a mediator between God and humans, (2) to deal gently with imperfect and uninformed parishioners, (3) to be a person of genuine humility, and (4) to be called into the priesthood by God. The next six verses then show how Christ's personality and ministry fit these qualifications to perfection.

In New Testament usage, being perfect is not an abstract idea. It does not refer to an aloof, out-of-touch person who never does anything wrong. We are not talking about having every hair in place and no spaghetti smears on a tie. In this biblical context, it means rather that Jesus perfectly fulfilled God's will, that he faithfully carried out God's plans and purposes. By this definition, Jesus was the perfect high priest because he was totally selfless. He talked very little about himself, about his own needs and accomplishments. He certainly did not glorify himself. J. Harry Cotton wrote, "Jesus owned no property, had not a place to lay his head (Luke 9:58), organized no institution to be his lengthened shadow, marshaled no resources, and at the end committed his gospel to a little group of unpromising men."[1] By being free of self, Jesus was able to fill his life with God's will and to be totally obedient, even unto death on the cross.

The person who composed this Letter to the Hebrews likens Jesus' role as high priest to that of Melchizedek, a king and priest in the time of Abraham and Sarah. Melchizedek was the priest who blessed Abraham, the father of the nation; who received ten percent of everything Abraham had; and who was considered superior to the Levitical priests who inherited their position. Melchizedek was ordained apparently not by human lineage but from on high by God (Genesis 14:17-20). So, too, was Jesus. Recall his baptism in which the voice of God is heard to say from heaven, "You are my Son, the Beloved; with you I am well pleased" (Luke 3:22b). Or again at the Transfiguration when God affirmed Jesus with these words: "This is my Son, my Chosen; listen to him!" (Luke 9:35).

Jesus is able to minister to us because he identifies so completely with our human condition. In his humanity, Jesus was not exempt from suffering and pain. When he prayed, he did so "with loud cries and tears" (Hebrews 5:7). Because he was one of us, Christ can serve as our priest with infinite patience and caring. Jesus genuinely experienced life. He did not waltz through his days on earth but truly felt everything we feel. He learned to be obedient to God through suffering, thereby becoming our source of eternal salvation.

It would appear that even for God's Son, suffering was an important and effective teacher. It certainly is for the rest of us humans. We are often slow to pay attention to the deep things of life or to learn our spiritual lessons, especially when things are comfortable. Times of abundance and ease seem to produce inward lethargy. Suffering perhaps helps to produce the humility and receptivity so necessary for learning and growth to occur.

Hebrews 6:1 quite succinctly explains what our response is to be as followers of Christ, our High Priest: "So come on, let's leave behind the preschool fingerpainting exercises on Christ and get on with the grand work of art. Grow up in Christ."[2]

What is it about the human race that makes it difficult for you to be truly selfless?

When in your life has suffering or deprivation taught you an invaluable truth?

When have you experienced a strength you never had before?

What "grand work of art" is on the easel of your life right now?

YOU CAN SPROUT OR YOU CAN MOLD
John 12:20-33

These few verses in John 12 recount a significant event in the "Jesus Movement." Would this new faith remain a seed in the national soil of Israel; or would it break open and sprout, expanding into the rest of the world? This was a crucial issue in the early church as well. Should the familiar and comfortable circle be opened to non-Jews, to Greeks and other Gentiles? Should the good news of Jesus Christ be the exclusive property of a few, or was it time to take it on the road? Biblical scholar William Barclay writes that this encounter with the Greeks in Jerusalem was "the first faint hint of a gospel which is to go out to all the world."[3] It would be fair to add, I think, that this issue must be addressed by every generation of Christians. The church in every age must decide whether to be a members-only club or a mission-oriented, witnessing band of believers.

The Greeks of Jesus' day were world-class travelers. Those who had the necessary time and resources constantly tried to experience new places and to discover new truths. During the Passover festival in Jerusalem there were always many pilgrims from around the world seeking to deepen their spiritual lives. Several Greeks requested an audience with Jesus. Perhaps they had heard about how he brought Lazarus back from the dead and may also have witnessed Jesus' triumphal entry. They wanted to spend quality time with Jesus, possibly intending to become his followers. So they approached Philip and made their request.

Philip was not certain what to say. The Master was a busy person, and these were extremely stressful days. Philip easily could have brushed off these inquiring souls with a quick no. They were strangers after all. But he made a wise decision. He consulted with Andrew whose opinions he must have valued, and together they went to ask Jesus. How often in our lives is the most helpful course of action that of confiding in a trusted friend or family member. Not only is there courage in numbers, there is spiritual wisdom as well.

Philip and Andrew may have anticipated a simple answer to their question from Jesus. Always one to teach whenever opportunities arose, however, Jesus chose instead to share a radically new and profound truth with them. He began by referring to himself as the Son of Man, a term from the Book of Daniel and interpreted by the Jews as a powerful person sent by God to free them from Roman domination. They assumed this representative of God would be mighty and would employ military force to accomplish this goal. But Jesus took those popular expectations and turned them upside down. Only when we bury our personal aims and desires, he said, do we become useful and productive persons. By yielding our own ambitions, we yield a fruitful harvest. Philip and Andrew's jaws must have dropped as they listened to this shocking message. "Do you mean to say, Jesus, it is by giving our lives away that we save them; by generously spending ourselves that we find life's riches?" This was exactly what he meant.

Once upon a time there was a pretty little grain of wheat. She was shiny and golden and rather shapely, too. Life on the shelf was quite pleasant, very clean and tidy with ample time for preening. She enjoyed the envious glances of the skinny carrot seeds and the shriveled up peas. She had heard disturbing rumors concerning the destiny of all seeds. "Perhaps," she mused, "other less beauteous kernels shall be buried beneath the dirt; but surely not I."

The season of fall arrived. In the fields the stubble had been turned under and disked. The refreshing autumn rains had soaked deeply into the rich soil. One day a farmer came to the store to buy winter wheat seed. "O, my!"

exclaimed the little grain, "this can't be happening to me. I'm in a sack. I'm in the bed of a bumpy old truck. Now I'm in a seed drill. Woe is me!"

Beneath the dark ground, she pouted. "Look at all this dirt. It's disgusting. I'm a filthy mess. Well, just because I've been planted doesn't mean I have to sprout. And I won't!" She watched in dismay as other seeds cracked apart and sent delicate shoots upward. "No way am I going to allow my gorgeous body to split open." By and by, however, she noticed an alarming, slimy discoloration on her perfect complexion. "Help me!" she cried. "Whatever shall I do?"

A wise kernel nearby replied. "My dear, you have but two choices: either sprout or mold. If you seek to save your life, you will surely lose it. You'll rot right where you lie. But if you'll crack open that hard outer shell, you shall grow until by next summer you'll be a graceful golden stalk bringing forth an abundant harvest."

Through the centuries theologians have devised various explanations of how this spending of self can result in a rich harvest. For example, theories of the Atonement have been formulated to describe the way Jesus' suffering and death provide for our salvation. The "Ransom Theory" assumes that humans are held hostage by sin. A price had to be paid to set us free. It required the most costly payment of all time:

the life of God's own Son. The "Substitutionary Model" explains that though we deserve to be punished for our sins, God sent Jesus to take our place. He who was without sin bore the brunt of our sin on the cross. He did not deserve such treatment; but out of his great love for us, he willingly gave his life. The "Moral Influence Theory" is based on our need for someone to show us the way. We look therefore to Jesus, our eternal role model, and are motivated to be and to do our best and to love one another. Another explanation might be called the "Reconciliation Model." Jesus lived and died to open the channels of God's grace and to enable us to live together in love with all our sisters and brothers: "Whoever serves me must follow me, and where I am, there will my servant be also" (John 12:26). Six verses later, Jesus adds these words: "And I, when I am lifted up from the earth, will draw all people to myself" (John 12:32). In Jesus' death and resurrection, we are drawn into the very essence of divine love and by implication are included in a community of believers. We are a reconciled and reconciling people.

I personally like what I call the "Humpty Dumpty Model." Everyone who saw Humpty after the fall noticed only his brokenness and tried unsuccessfully to fix it. They should instead have put him to the use for which God created him and made an omelet to feed hungry people, for it is in our brokenness that we are able to nourish others. It is in cracking open the hard shell around our hearts that we are able to love. It is in dying that we are made new, born to eternal life.

What human factors cause you to resist expanding the circle of your fellowship and to be slow to welcome newcomers graciously?

How long has it been since you checked your soul for any spots of mildew or mold?

How many new faith sprouts do you see?

What kinds of fruits will they someday produce?

---

[1]From *The Interpreter's Bible, Vol. 11*; page 643.

[2]From *The Message*; page 463.

[3]From *The Daily Bible Study Series, Gospel of John, Vol. 2*; page 120.

Trust and Obey

Scriptures for Lent:
The Sixth Sunday
Isaiah 50:4-9a
Philippians 2:5-11
Mark 15:1-39

Apple trees in north central Washington produce an extremely high quality fruit. Apples grown in this area are famous around the world for their taste and crispness. Red Delicious, Granny Smiths, Galas, and a host of other varieties stay fresh up to a year when kept in a controlled atmospheric method of storage. Along with proper soil and adequate water supplies, the climate is a crucial element in producing such excellence. Weather conditions are often severe enough to cause the trees themselves to struggle mightily. In any given season, they may have a tough time surviving. Summer temperatures are frequently too hot, and the cold of winter may dip low enough to damage their root systems. Consequently, apple trees do not waste energy on producing an over abundance of foliage. Looking beautiful is not as important to them as being fruitful. Experiencing deprivation helps the orchards nestled in the valleys to focus on their true reason for existence. Their suffering becomes a source of transformation, turning potential defeats into blessings by which they provide nourishment for the world, thus fulfilling their Creator's purpose.

The prophet Isaiah experienced numerous struggles in his life. Many of the common people and a number of political leaders chose to reject the heart of his message. Yet in wonderfully poetic ways, he continued to prophesy. His words were a call to remain steadfast in times of conflict, to stay positive and hopeful when criticized, to be determined and faithful in the face of suffering. Tradition has it that Isaiah met a violent end. Yet he was one who proclaimed the coming of the Prince of Peace (Isaiah 9:6) and who anticipated a day when "the wolf shall live with the lamb, / the leopard shall lie down with the kid, / the calf and the lion and the fatling together, / and a little child shall lead them" (Isaiah 11:6).

Before a pitcher can be filled with fresh, sparkling water, it must first be totally emptied of all its stale or stagnant contents. In like manner, wrote Paul in this Sunday's lection, Jesus emptied himself of all claims to equality with God in order to be the source of our salvation. We, then, the recipients of his grace, are challenged to have this mind of Christ within us; that is, we are to embody in our lives the attitudes and disposition of Christ.

At first reading, the Gospel passage seems to imply that Jesus was the victim of political forces and intrigue, the scapegoat of religious leaders and their jealousy, the pawn of Pontius Pilate and his pandering to the crowd, at the mercy of the fickle loyalties of those throngs packing the Jerusalem streets during the Passover festival. It was not the case. Jesus chose this moment. It was the culmination of approximately three years of vital ministry and the answer to intense prayer in the garden of Gethsemane. He was no victim. His life was not taken from him. His silence before his accusers was not a sign of weakness but of incredible strength and courage. Jesus gave his life for us and for all humanity that we might be forgiven and made whole, that we might have the hope of and be fit for eternity.

GRACE UNDER FIRE
Isaiah 50:4-9a

The older I get the more of an individual I become. I do not much care anymore who I impress. I wear clothes for their comfort, not their style. I go to restaurants where the food is good and the prices reasonable rather than to be seen in some trendy establishment. I own a big four-wheel drive pickup and go around with the windows rolled down while playing loud classical music in a mostly country-western kind of town. You have to know from these Old Testament verses that Isaiah was very much his own person, too. He said what needed to be said. He did often wax eloquent; he had a marvelously lyrical quality to his words. Yet he never lost sight of the fact that he was God's prophet to the nation Israel.

Isaiah understood his role to be that of a teacher and an encourager of people: "The Lord GOD has given me the tongue of a teacher, / that I may know how to sustain the weary with a word" (Isaiah 50:4). Not only did he speak clearly and with wisdom, he listened intently for the voice of God. Such a gifted person with language was this eighth century B.C. prophet.

We have the benefit in today's world of numerous books, videos, and workshops on how to manage conflict, on the most effective methods for resolving disagreements. Isaiah had to cope with conflict in his life without such blessings. Yet he did well. First of all, he listened. He seemed to know intuitively that a good teacher must be a good listener.

He was quite obviously open to fresh concepts and receptive to innovative ideas. Isaiah dared to go against the dominant theology of the day that believed the Messiah would come as a conquering, military hero. Isaiah understood that this Chosen One would instead be revealed by God as a suffering servant (Isaiah 53).

We, too, would be well-advised to practice the art of listening. In our fast-paced society crammed with activities and filled with noise, moments of quietness are to be cherished. It may be that God, who spoke to Elijah in the "sound of sheer silence" (1 Kings 19:11-12), still speaks to us in whispers that we hear only when our souls are hushed and attentive. This text from Isaiah is a marvelous example of the way God shares eternal truth with the minds and hearts of truly receptive individuals and with communities of faith who create ample opportunities for quietness and patient waiting.

Isaiah also possessed the fruits of courage and endurance. His adversaries may have thought him stubborn. Perhaps they were right; but if so, it was a gift bestowed on him by God. He would not yield what he knew to be everlastingly true. He trusted and obeyed.

God called Isaiah into the prophetic ministry in a dramatic moment (Isaiah 6). He may well have been a Temple priest when he experienced this powerful moving of the Spirit in his life. Smoke filled the house of the Lord, and angelic creatures hovered close by. Isaiah was in awe of God's might and was led to humbly confess his own unworthiness. He received forgiveness when a seraph touched his lips with a live coal, a burning ember brought from the altar. Out of the smoke came the voice of God asking, "Whom shall I send, and who will go for us?" Isaiah responded instantly, "Here am I; send me" (6:8).

Completely convinced of his prophetic calling, Isaiah stood firm when human voices were raised in opposition. These verses in Chapter 50 may have been a reflection on his own suffering at the hands of his detractors. Yet he also knew that when the Messiah came, this person would be steadfast in fulfilling the purposes of God. There would be no running away or hiding from conflict. The Suffering Servant would willingly accept the abuse and feel the pain, not only outwardly and physically but inwardly and spiritually. In the midst of such humiliation, the Servant of God would maintain a flint-like face and reveal a look of absolute determination. The Servant would trust and obey. This would be no easy task considering the intensely personal and degrading nature of the attacks. He would face insults and be spat upon; his beard (a badge of faithfulness to God) would be pulled out one hair at a time. Nevertheless, there would be no retaliation. Rather than attempting to flee or trying to inflict pain in return, he would express total trust in God: "I know that I shall not be put to shame; / he who vindicates me is near" (50:7c-8a).

I can only hope when conflicts come my way, as surely they will, that by the grace of God I will be inspired by God's Suffering Servant to deal with them squarely and to manage them creatively. "It is the Lord GOD who helps me," wrote the prophet (50:9). We can handle the toughest situations when we stand together with God. It is an unbeatable combination: God's loving support and our human perseverance. We need look no further for evidence than to the heroes and heroines of the faith. From Stephen to Paul, from Francis of Assisi to Joan of Arc, from Martin Luther King, Jr. to Mother Teresa, we can see a great parade of saints who have claimed God's promises and who have courageously, steadfastly moved toward them. Along with countless other souls, these are people who have understood that suffering is not a penalty, not a punishment from God, but rather an opportunity for God's redemptive purposes to be fulfilled. Most of us do not go through life looking for trouble, dissention, or conflict. When it does occur, with God's help we can not only endure, we can discover in it the hope of deeper faith, renewed strength, and transformation.

If you were a teacher, what grade would you give yourself for how well you listen to the Word and the messages of God? to the joys and struggles of your friends and family? to the voices of children and youth around you?

When have you found it possible to sing "nobody knows the trouble I see," yet shout "glory hallelujah"?

How has God given you hope in times of trouble, dissention, or conflict?

LET ME BE EMPTIED
Philippians 2:5-11

I'm a collector. Just take a look in our garage or ask my spouse. She has lived with it for nearly forty years. I hoard baseball cards, old bottles and books, wooden thread spools, and glass doorknobs. You name it, and I probably collect it. It is not a particularly bad habit other than the clutter that results. When we clutter up our inner lives, our souls, with dusty old ideas, moldy beliefs, and a stale faith, however, it can become a major spiritual problem. Our faith must always be green and growing. When we fill our lives with nothing but past experiences and familiar people, we are in danger of losing sight of the fresh ways God seeks to relate to us. We risk having parched spirits and hardened hearts.

The name of the game is to keep the movement of the Spirit going continuously, to be filled to overflowing by God's love and to pour it out on a needy world.

Then we are to repeat the process over and over until that final outpouring we call death and our eternal refilling in glory. Our human tendency is to grab hold of whatever blessings come our way and to not let go. We huddle with people we already know rather than expand our circle of love to welcome strangers or to include newcomers and the lonely. We become set in our ways and are resistant to new ideas and creative approaches to old problems. We prefer what is comfortable and predictable. This has the potential of turning us into rigid and inflexible people.

The source of our comfort is not anything we can grasp, tuck away in a safety deposit box, or permanently place in a human container of any kind. We are talking about God's Spirit that moves like water and blows like wind, flits like a butterfly and soars like the eagle. That same spontaneous, creative, free Spirit has no desire to turn into concrete in our brains. This boundless energy of God simply will not become our personal property or our private domain. The Holy Spirit is God's gift for all time and all people. It will not hold still long enough for a nation, a denomination, a congregation, or an individual to claim as its own. It cannot ever be corralled.

The lives of those who would be Jesus' disciples are about being filled and emptied, emptied and filled. Paul wrote that Christ Jesus, though he was in the form of God, never claimed the privileges that went with this exalted status. He instead "emptied himself, taking the form of a slave, being born in human likeness" (Philippians 2:7). The Greek verb translated "to empty" means to pour out a liquid to the very last droplet, until the container is totally void. Jesus did exactly that on the cross, giving himself completely for the sake of humanity. It was a gift of great humility and pure love. It is as though "God has given us a love transfusion by the Holy Spirit" (Romans 5:5, The Cotton Patch Version).

Jesus offers this spiritual transfusion to every person regardless of their outward circumstances. He emptied himself for all humanity, not just for the wealthy, beautiful, and successful; not even for those who faithfully sit in church Sunday after Sunday. Our Savior is available to the whole world. In his earthly ministry he reached out to people based on their need, not their worthiness. He noticed and loved regular folks like you and me.

Several years ago I officiated at the wedding ceremony for a bride and groom from two prominent families. Their rehearsal dinner was on the fiftieth floor of an elegant skyscraper. It was a sumptuous multi-course meal in which we moved from one beautiful room to another. As we dined together in the spacious library, however, I observed that the restaurant staff was invisible to most of the guests. Servers were seen only when they failed to move quickly enough or when they made a small mistake. There was no "thank you" when a job was done well, not so much as a quick nod or glance in their direction. My spouse and I felt out of place whenever we acknowledged their efficient service and pleasant demeanor. I am fairly certain the staff received a generous gratuity, and deservedly so. No amount of money can compensate for being ignored, however, for being treated as less than the wonderful, special children of God we truly are.

Like Jesus, God expects us to empty ourselves for the sake of the world: "Let the same mind be in you that was in Christ Jesus" (Philippians 2:5). We are to spend our personalities freely and generously on others; to give our love, time, energy, and financial resources; to offer our best wishes and prayers. We are not to save ourselves for a rainy day, nor postpone serving the world until the sweet by and by, nor sit on our blessed assurances expecting others to fulfill our ministry for us. Our patterns of thinking and disposition are to be based on the mind and life of Christ. Like Christ, we are to empty ourselves, trust God, and obey.

You and I would do well to begin our prayers with a request that God first empty us before asking for every good and perfect gift. "Empty me, O God, of wanting my own way in order to open me to your word and will. Free me from defending my little piece of turf that I may embrace the world. Empty me of all my insignificant and petty habits that I may experience the fullness of your joy. Let me pour out all of my self-importance and be refilled with childlike honesty and humility. Empty me of my narrow attitudes that I might gain true wisdom. Cleanse me of all partial commitments that I may be enthusiastic about being your servant. Drain from me the last drop of conditional, restrictive love, then replenish my soul until I love you with all my heart and mind and soul and strength."

John Wesley offered this profound prayer as part of his Covenant Service. I commend it to you for inclusion in your regular life of prayer.

Let me be your servant, under
    your command.
I will no longer be my own.
I will give up myself to your will in
    all things.
. . . .
Lord, make me what you will.
I put myself fully into your hands:
    put me to doing, put me to suf-
        fering,
    let me be employed for you, or
        laid aside for you,
    let me be full, let me be empty,
    let me have all things, let me
        have nothing.
I freely and with a willing heart
    give it all to your pleasure and
        disposal. Amen.[1]

What thoughts, views, and dispositions in your life need to be emptied?

Can you think of any people or groups in your area who for all practical purposes are "invisible" to others? What factors may contribute to this unwholesome attitude?

In what ways would our society be reshaped if all Christians truly had the mind of Christ and lived accordingly each day?

THE BEST DEFENSE IS A GOOD OFFENSE
Mark 15:1-39

One of our sons loved playing high school football. He was short of stature but used his quickness and true grit in his position as starting nose tackle. There in the middle of the defensive line, surrounded by young men, was our little boy. His mother and I were proud that he was a team captain, but it was still difficult to watch him play because he was often a hundred or more pounds lighter and a foot shorter than his opponents. Pound for pound he was probably one of the best athletes on the field; and he played with fire in his eyes. Nevertheless, we liked the games better when the offense had the ball and our son was safe on the bench. No giant guards or tackles could flatten him there. He did not much enjoy benchsitting and would nervously pace the sidelines until the coach sent him back in.

After the games, I often reminded our son of an old football adage: "The best defense is a good offense." We had some lively but friendly disagreements over the truth of that statement. I could have told him it was biblical, but that would have been preaching. What teenager wants to hear a sermon from his or her dad? My text, however, would have been from the Letter to the Romans: "Take the offensive—overpower evil by good!" (Romans 12:21, J.B. Phillips).

Our Gospel passage from Mark 15 expresses what Jesus' game plan was during the last days of his life on earth. He took the offensive. With prayer and courage, he made his move. The time was right for him to confront the issues, so he set his face toward Jerusalem. When his dear friend Lazarus died, Jesus and his small band traveled to Bethany, a small village on the outskirts of the Holy City. Reviving Lazarus after he had been four days in the tomb only aggravated the authorities more. It also served to enhance Jesus' popularity with the people and increase his visibility.

Following that miracle, the events leading up to Jesus' death happened rather quickly. After Jesus' betrayal, he appeared almost immediately before the chief priests, the elders, the scribes, and the entire Jewish council, known as the Sanhedrin. They handed him over to Pontius Pilate, the Roman procurator, who alone had power to order the death penalty.

In a cursory reading of this passage, it may seem as though Jesus is on the defensive. He is almost completely silent before his accusers, replying to Pilate's question as to whether he was king of the Jews with three terse words, "You say so" (Mark 15:2b). Do not, however, mistake Jesus' quietness for passivity. He is on the offensive. He is expressing God's wondrous love for humanity by his suffering and death. It is the fulfillment of Isaiah's suffering servant prophecies. It results in Jesus pouring out his life for us, emptying himself on the cross for our salvation.

Jesus employed the power of silence throughout his entire ordeal. The contrast is striking between the calmness and peace within Jesus and the anxiety and turmoil of his tormenters. Pilate and the others do not take his life. He gives himself to a hurting and lost world (John 10:17-18).

Mark's graphic account of Jesus' passion—his trial, the mocking and abuse, his crucifixion and death—pierce our hearts even as the nails pierced his hands and feet. We prefer to skip over these verses and to proceed directly from Palm Sunday's victory celebration to the joy of Easter's resurrection. But the road to new life goes directly through this passion narrative. There is no scenic route, no shortcut.

You and I experience in very small ways something of this same tension. We dare not compare what we endure to Jesus' sacrifice, yet our struggles are real to us and significant to the heart of God. We may experience rejection because of our faith; we are hurt because of how much we love; we are disappointed because we are a people of great hope. I remember many a late night conversation with my spouse, discussing her role as a minister's wife. The particular issues changed from time to time, but the conclusions always seemed to be the same. "I don't like being taken advantage of just because I'm married to you," she'd say as we wearily nodded off to sleep. "So before they ask, I'm going to volunteer. That way I'll never feel used. It will be my decision, a gift from me to them." So it was with Jesus' passion. His suffering and death were gifts of love.

The love nailed on that rough cross bore immediate results. The Roman centurion who was in charge of the Crucifixion became the first Gentile to witness to the divinity of Jesus: "Truly this man was God's Son!" (Mark 15:39). Jesus gave no lengthy discourse to this career soldier. There was no pulpit pounding or altar call. By his courageous suffering and his quiet, unwavering love, Jesus touched this person's soul.

Down through the centuries that have followed, variations of this theme have been repeated again and again, of how one loving person by taking the offensive changed the entire world. Surely we in the contemporary church have clear hints from God of what this text means for our work together. Could it be that our success will not come by hype, improved public relations, bigger budgets, the latest technology, or even theological correctness? It is in proclaiming Christ and him crucified, by tenderly caring for and unconditionally loving others and giving them hope, by trusting and obeying, that seekers will be brought into the realm of God.

When you have been used by others, how did you feel? Were you able to find positive and creative ways to resolve the dilemma? Why or why not?

How can quietness be assertive and serve as an effective witness for Jesus Christ?

What is it about silence that allows creative possibilities to emerge?

What personal attributes and qualities are necessary in order for someone to take the offensive for God yet not be offensive to others?

When have you taken the offensive for God?

[1]From *The Book of Worship* (The United Methodist Publishing House, 1992); page 291.

Running to the Resurrection

Scriptures for Easter Day:
Acts 10:34-43
1 Corinthians 15:1-11
John 20:1-18

"Grandpa, play chase with me! Please! It's been three days since we have, and you know how much I like to run." Five-year-old Ashley does love to run. If I fail to respond quickly to her request, her voice becomes louder and more insistent: "Grandpa! Start running." Away I go around the backyard swing set, past our weather-beaten picnic table, huffing and puffing, to crouch behind the wooden fence. She catches me; so I'm off again, this time through the gate into the front yard where I circle the old maple tree with Ashley in hot pursuit. It is a great game; but I must admit I breathe a sigh of relief when her mother, our daughter, comes to pick up her children. My legs are longer than Ashley's, but they are also fifty-three years older. So are my muscles and lungs. After a few minutes on the sofa, I am refreshed and ready to go again. I am actually very grateful for God's gift of grandchildren. They keep us grandparents enthusiastic about life and young at heart.

So, too, did that first Easter morning infuse those participants with hope and joy. The followers of Jesus had moped about for three days, looking sad and downcast. Their beloved leader had died and been buried. They were in shock and felt totally lost. Some huddled in fear back in the upper room. Others scuffled home down a dusty road to the village of Emmaus. Before dawn, Mary Magdalene went to the burial site, slowly making her way through the darkness. When she discovered the empty tomb, the running around began. She raced back to tell Simon Peter and the beloved disciple. These two got into a foot race in their haste to check out Mary's report. Peter, perhaps older and stockier, came in second. But run he did! So did the Emmaus travelers, who once their companion was revealed to them as the Risen Christ, returned at full speed to Jerusalem.

When Easter day arrived, the

pace of Jesus' little band of intimate disciples quickened. They seemed to be running everywhere. We who are Christ's people today are not expected to run to the sunrise service, jog to church, and then sprint to brunch. It might be healthier if we did, rather than walking or driving sedately; but it would surely mess up our hairdos and leave our new clothes looking disheveled. Those original disciples did not care one whit about outward appearances, however. They were so filled with excitement, so enthusiastic and energized, they could not hold still. Maybe I should race granddaughters Ashley and her little sister Alexis to worship this Easter morn; and instead of arriving all prim and proper, have my heart racing, be breathless, and thus experience a tumult of hope and joy.

The Acts of the Apostles, which chronicles the events of the church's birth and infancy, certainly gets off to a running start too. Peter may have been physically panting hard when he got to the tomb on Easter, but that was nothing compared to what followed in the next few weeks. From Pentecost through our lection in Acts 10, Jesus' followers are described as being caught in a spiritual whirlwind. The story culminates in Peter's radically altered attitude concerning the direction of their common ministry. In a vision of spectacular proportions (Acts 10:9-16), Peter is convinced to lead the early believers from being members of a Jewish cult into becoming participants in a rapidly growing, world-encircling movement.

Paul, who arrived on the scene somewhat late, still managed to get in on the excitement. It does not really matter when you come on board. Whether you are first up the gangplank or are running late and have to jump off the dock as the ship embarks, you are a full member of the crew. Paul may not have been with Jesus from the beginning, but we certainly cannot question his zeal or enthusiasm for sharing the gospel. First Corinthians 15 is one of the greatest explanations and affirmations of the Resurrection ever composed. If I were to assign any Easter homework, this would be it—reading Chapter 15 in its entirety. The specific verses for this Sunday introduce the Resurrection theme by presenting a thumbnail history of that event followed by a brief and humble sketch of Paul's credentials.

When we arrive at our Gospel lesson, we can feel the excitement rising. Our pace quickens, and our respiration increases. For Christians, this is the most amazing and dramatic moment in the entire history of our planet. Quite naturally we have adopted the practice of arising early to greet the dawn, of thronging together with our extended church family for worship, and of trying to retain the Resurrection's glow a little longer by joining others for brunch. We want to squeeze every bit of joy and hope we can out of our annual Easter experience. Nor is Easter a one-time event. It is intended to be a lifelong adventure of faith. So we might as well put on our running shoes and "run with perseverance the race that is set before us" (Hebrews 12:1).

A QUANTUM LEAP OF FAITH
Acts 10:34-43

At times in history God has acted decisively; people's beliefs and society's structures have been radically and quickly changed. The Book of Acts describes just such a period with one surprising thing happening after another. These events would be wonderful material for a great action movie. In Chapter 1, the Risen Christ ascends to heaven, setting the stage for the coming of the Holy Spirit on the Day of Pentecost some fifty days after Easter. The Spirit comes suddenly with a sound like a violent wind. Tongues of flame, indicating the power and warmth of God's indwelling presence, rest over the heads of each person gathered there in Jerusalem. The worshipers come from every corner of the earth and speak various languages, yet they are able to communicate clearly with one another. This "birthday of the church" provides the impetus for future growth: "Day by day the Lord added to their number those who were being saved" (Acts 2:47b). These truly were stirring times.

Next, Peter and John heal a man who has been lame from birth (Acts 3). You may recall Peter's words: "I have no silver or gold, but what I have I give you; in the name of Jesus Christ of Nazareth, stand up and walk" (3:6). Peter and John are subsequently arrested for speaking boldly to the people, then are released with orders to stop talking about Jesus. They will not be silenced, however, and together with other believers simply pray for more courage and greater boldness.

As the church's numbers increase, so does the workload. Seven wise and caring persons, including Stephen, are appointed to help the disciples fulfill their responsibilities. The story goes on: Stephen is stoned to death by an angry mob for his eloquent but blunt witness (Chapter 7); Philip preaches in Samaria and baptizes an Ethiopian court official (Chapter 8); Saul is converted on the Damascus road (Chapter 9).

By the time we get to Chapter 10, we need a pause to catch our breath. It will not happen, though; for here we encounter what might be called a quantum leap of faith. Peter and other leaders believe that to be Christian, a person must first become Jewish. Then Peter receives a vision from God. Its purpose is to convince Peter to take a completely new look at how converts come to Christ. The vision is about clean and unclean foods, but at a far deeper level it is about God's desire for the church to be all-inclusive. Peter is asked to let go of his own tightly held agenda in order to embrace the will of God. To Peter's credit, he does so gracefully and with little resistance.

Our text from Acts forms the essence of Peter's sermon to Cornelius, a Roman centurion, his relatives, and his close friends, all Gentiles. As with preachers of every century and culture, Peter includes himself as needing to hear the message. His first words are, "I truly understand that God shows no partiality, but in every nation anyone who fears him and does what is right is acceptable to him" (10:34-35). The souls of his listeners are changed and made new. But so is Peter's heart and mind. Shortly after this breakthrough of the Spirit, the church explodes into every corner of the world.

I can only hope that we Christians, who are making our first tentative steps into the twenty-first century and the third millennium, will in some small way have the same courage Peter had. It seems that God is expecting and encouraging the church today to make a quantum leap in its thinking and the way it goes about its business. We are being called to present the gospel with fresh and contemporary methods. We are being asked to sing new songs to the Lord; to employ exciting media tools and technology to reach younger generations for Christ; to move away from dependence on ordained, professional clergy to a deep involvement of laity in the whole life of the church. Local and global missions are being viewed as integral to every church's ministry, not just as line items in the budget but as hands-on, person-to-person sharing. It is both an exciting and unsettling time for church members. This God who shows no partiality, who plays no favorites, is pushing us out the doors of our buildings and into our communities.

There can be no mistaking the message. God will not permit us to operate exclusive country club congregations or members only institutions. Just as God nudged the first century church, so is God urging the twenty-first century church out of its complacency. If we fail to respond to God's gentle nudging, soon we will be feeling a more forceful and insistent divine shoving. The Holy Spirit is an ever-moving, continuously creating presence. Perhaps it is the restless, brooding nature of God who simply will not let us have closed minds and uncaring hearts, who sends us forth with tidings of hope for the world.

What steps might we take to correct our closed-mindedness, our stubborn adherence to our own small agendas, our tendency to exclude others who are different from us?

When have you had "out of the blue" or "quantum leap" experiences in your beliefs about God or the church?

When have you had similar experiences in other areas of your life, such as your work or profession, your family and friendships?

When you are truly receptive and spiritually in tune, what do you hear the Holy Spirit saying to you personally?

THE TRUTH BEARS REPEATING
1 Corinthians 15:1-11

My father was quite a storyteller. He had an amazing number of stories tucked in his brain and could always seem to find one to fit every occasion. There was only one minor problem. He repeated them, not just once but in multiples. The older he got, the more he recycled his tales, anecdotes, and jokes. Since everybody loved and respected him, we forgave him, pretending it was the first time we had ever heard that saga.

I must confess, however, that I was not always patient and kind with his proclivity for repetition. When I was a high school youth, I sang baritone in the church choir. Papa was the preacher. The choir sat in the chancel area facing the congregation. Mama always sat in the second pew, directly in front of the pulpit. She was papa's number one fan and head cheerleader—with one notable exception. During the sermon, if either Mama or

I had heard him use an illustration before, we would secretly signal the other. I would rub my nose with two fingers. She would run three fingers through her hair to indicate it was not the second time he had shared that story in this particular church; it was the third. She and I enjoyed our little game immensely.

Papa was a good sport but not as amused as we were, especially when we would continue our friendly debate over Sunday lunch. He would try to convince us it was the first time he had ever told that story; and one of us would say, "Then how come I've got the punch line memorized?"

We may have given him a bad time, but Papa was right. The truth bears repeating. If something is profoundly important and everlastingly true, we need to hear it over and over again in order to fix it in our minds. It helps us realize how vital God's Word is for our well-being. For example, the Hebrew people knew how crucial God's commandments were to their existence; so they frequently recited them to their children (Deuteronomy 7–9). You can never tell each other too often about the laws and the love of God.

Paul realized this fact. His writing in 1 Corinthians 15 is a refresher course of what Jesus Christ means to us: "I would remind you, brothers and sisters, of the good news that I proclaimed to you" (1 Corinthians 15:1). He proceeds to lay out the basics of our faith: that Christ died in accordance with the Scriptures, was buried and then resurrected three days later, appeared as the Risen Christ to various individuals, and "last of all, as to one untimely born, he appeared also to [Paul]" (15:3-8).

Returning to the basics of our faith is a healthy practice for even the most mature of Christian disciples. Just as rehearsals are necessary for plays and weddings, so are they of value for firming up our religious beliefs and making solid our biblical grounding. I would have been a far better violinist as a youngster had I practiced and rehearsed more instead of playing marbles with my buddies. These days my faith would be deeper and wider if I studied and reviewed God's Word more and played computer solitaire less.

I need to be reminded frequently of those relationships and realities that truly matter in my life. I suppose that is the reason for special occasions such as Valentine's Day; mother's, father's, and grandparent's days; the Fourth of July; Thanksgiving; and other celebrations like birthdays and anniversaries. We do not mean to forget. We simply get too busy with daily demands and activities and allow many of life's sweetest joys to be crowded out.

I think Paul also knew we humans need to practice and repeat our belief in Christ so that when crises come, as surely they will, we will be adequately prepared. It is always sad when

tragedy strikes anyone but doubly so when that person or family does not have a firm faith in God. Our relationship to Jesus Christ is not to be a once-in-a-while, when-it's-convenient-for-me kind of thing. We are blessed when we practice the presence of God day by day.

It is also true that if we want to share our faith with others, as we are instructed by Jesus to do, rehearsing what we believe is not only helpful, it is essential. Our witnessing is far more effective and winsome when we have considered our faith and seriously reflected about our spiritual lives. We have a story to tell to the nations and to our family, friends, and neighbors. We will be able to share it with power when we know it well, when it is deeply imbedded in our hearts and souls.

I rather think my papa is smiling down on me from heaven because I am carrying on with his tradition. I now tell the same story so many times I forget who has heard it and who has not. In my mature years I know something I but dimly grasped earlier—the truth, the tidings of hope, bears repeating.

How often do you practice and rehearse the basics of your faith in God? What things distract or prevent you from practicing more?

How has your faith in Christ sustained you in times of trouble?

What preparations are you presently making to increase your spiritual strength in order to endure future crises?

I HAVE SEEN THE LORD!
John 20:1-18

Some years ago I had the privilege of reading several sections from a man's journal in planning for his memorial service. His account of what he did on Easter Sunday, 1996, touched my soul. I hope this excerpt from Hans's experience that day might speak to your hearts as it did to mine.

I awoke this morning when the sky was barely waking. Today is a special day. As I left the house by the side door, the little birds who live in the bush next to it were softly chirping to let me know I woke them up. By the time I reached the high place in the mountains from where I can overlook the whole valley, the light of day had lifted over the rim but the sun was not yet up. There was a cloud formation above the rimrock to the east with a golden lining on the underside that intensified gradually. While waiting for the sun to rise, I read about Mary Magdalene finding the sepulchre empty and running to tell Simon Peter and John they had taken the Lord away; and when Jesus said to her, "I am ascending to my Father and to your Father, to my God and your God." The sun rose over the rim and lit up the clouds, creating a most wonderful spectacle of radiating light. It was a glorious setting to commemorate the ascent of Christ to heaven to sit at his Father's side, nearly two thousand years ago. A little robin was sitting on a post off to the side all this time, as if waiting with me to see the sunrise. I reminded myself that he was also one of God's creations. Maybe it was a sign that my prayer had reached heaven. When the little robin flew away, I too left for home. Thank you, Lord, for a most beautiful Easter day.

I contrast Hans's mountaintop moment that year with my own Easter activities. I was down in the valley below, scurrying about anxiously; making certain the church doors were unlocked, the lights on, the lilies watered, the bulletins all in place, the extra folding chairs in readiness. By the time morning was over, I was exhausted and my spirit frustrated. I had forgotten what Easter is really about. Its focus is not on outward things. Yes, someone needs to attend to the details of worship. But Easter is food for the hungry soul, tidings of hope. It is about walking slowly with Mary Magdalene in the dusk toward an empty tomb; about sprinting through the dewy morning grass with Peter and the disciple whom Jesus loved; about meeting the risen Christ in the garden and having him tenderly, lovingly speak your name.

I'm certain each of us at some point on Easter day wishes to exclaim with Mary, "I have seen the Lord" (John 20:18). (The biblical text is punctuated with a period. I think it should be an exclamation point: "I have seen the Lord!") It may happen as we sing the great Easter hymns in the congregation of God's people. It might occur in those precious moments of silent prayer and meditation. The Scripture readings or the sermon may be for us a special blessing. Perhaps it will be the strong fragrance of lilies or the sight of festive balloons or butterfly banners. Or, maybe you will whisper, "I have seen the Lord," as you hold a small child in your arms in the nursery. Whatever it is, be ready. Mary was not expecting to see Jesus that morning. But there he was, waiting for her. Though twenty centuries have come and gone, the Risen Christ is still waiting to greet you and me on the holiest of Christian days.

In a world where tragedy seems forever waiting just around the next corner and where injustice, violence, and grief seem to stalk us continuously, we need Easter's bright hope and fullness of joy. God has wonderfully created us human creatures. We come complete with an astounding range of feelings. One moment we are cautiously making our way through a valley of dark shadows; the next we are toe dancing on a mountaintop bathed in joyful light. Consider the emotional roller coaster those first followers had to endure. Mary Magdalene, for example, went from the numbness of grief and a night of quiet weeping to a sudden crescendo of joy in the early dawn. Simon Peter journeyed from the depths of shame and guilt to the hope of sharing breakfast on the shore with Christ and being given a second chance.

One wonders why Mary failed to recognize Jesus in the garden. Perhaps she was still in shock, too wrapped up in the cloak of sorrow. It is also possible, however, that Jesus appeared as a "plain clothes" Risen Christ. You would not mistake someone wearing flowing robes, bedecked in jewels, and crowned in gold for the gardener, now would you? I wonder if Jesus had been puttering in the garden as he waited for Mary; that maybe there was grime under his fingernails and mud on his sandals. This was the carpenter's son after all, the Word become flesh and blood and dirt.

What about you and me? How do we expect our Lord to come to us? Are we looking for a three-piece suit and silk tie, leather briefcase firmly in hand? Suppose Jesus appears to us and we mistake him for the cleaning lady in the kitchen, the man rocking back and forth in a nursing home, the child at play in a bare yard. We do not know the day or time of his appearing (Acts 1:6-7); nor apparently will we know exactly what our Lord will look like, either. We are in good company, of course. Even after being traveling companions on the road to Emmaus, the two followers did not recognize him. Thomas did not trust his eyes. He needed to touch in order to believe. Our responsibility is to be alert and ready. This God of hope and joy and new life is ever full of surprises.

You might say what happened to these ancient disciples was the first "joice;" and we who have followed in their footsteps have been re-joicing ever since. If so, we ought to be doing a better job of it. We should be turning cartwheels and doing pirouettes, jumping for joy, running pell-mell around our church buildings instead of sitting comfortably in cushioned pews. Rather than complaining, "There's no place to park in this lot" or "We're going to be late for brunch if we sing all six verses," we should be shouting with all the saints in glory: "Christ is risen! He is risen indeed!"

As Jesus and Mary said their farewell in the garden that Easter morn, Jesus told her not to hold on to him because he had not yet ascended to God. Mary wanted to grab hold and hug him for dear life. But this Gardener, who plants and prunes and waters souls, had risen from the grave not only for her. He is available for all people and all time, even for eternity. We, too, may exclaim, "I have seen the Lord!" We, too, may share the tidings of hope with the whole world.

How might Christians today fulfill God's call to rejoice and be exceedingly glad?

In what unexpected places and surprising ways have you encountered the presence of the Risen Christ?

What are some new ways you might express the tidings of hope present at Easter?   .

$\mathcal{M}$eet the Writer

Kel Groseclose is the Minister of Congregational Care at First United Methodist Church, Wenatchee, Washington. Kel is married to Ellen and the couple has lived in Wenatchee for twenty-five years. Their family, besides four cats, is comprised of six children and six beautiful grandchildren. A native of the Pacific Northwest and Alaska, Kel has studied at the University of Puget Sound, Boston University School of Theology, and San Francisco Theological Seminary.

Kel has written a weekly editorial column for the *Wenatchee World* for more than eleven years. He is the author of seven books including *Three Speed Dad in a Ten Speed World*, a humorous book about parenting; *This Too Shall Pass: Encouragement for Parents Who Sometimes Doubt Their Teenagers Were Created in the Image of God;* and two in the *Moment with God* series, one for men and another for grandparents.

Kel finds joy and relaxation in planting seeds and tending a garden, blowing soap bubbles with granddaughters, playing the old-time fiddle, writing in his journal, and being in God's great outdoors.